# Grand Canyon River Hikes

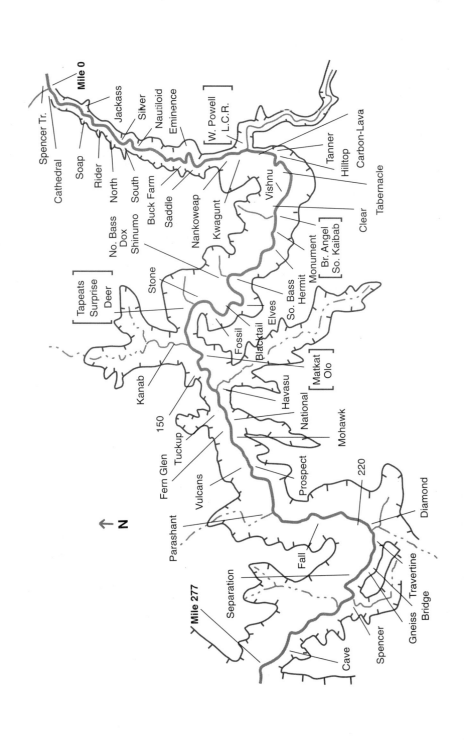

# Alphabetical List of Hikes

Edited by Ginny Gelczis, Bret Simmons
Designed by Mary Williams
Front cover photo by Lisa Gelczis
Back cover background photo by Dugald Bremner
All photos by author unless otherwise credited

# Grand Canyon River Hikes

Tyler Williams

Funhog Press

**River Permit Information**
River Permits Office
Grand Canyon National Park
PO Box 129
Grand Canyon, Arizona 86023
phone: 1-800-959-9164 or (520) 638-7843
fax: (520) 638-7844

**Navajo Nation**
Cameron Visitor Center
PO Box 549
Cameron, AZ 86020
phone: (520) 679-2303

**Navajo Parks and Recreation Department**
PO Box 9000
Window Rock, AZ 86515
phone: (520) 871-6647

**Hualapai Tribe**
phone: (520) 769-2219

Other titles from Funhog Press

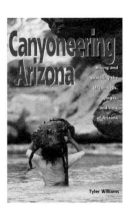

Canyoneering Arizona
ISBN 0-9664919-0-4
$18.95

# Table of Contents

# Disclaimer

Hiking is dangerous. Other dangerous activities commonly practiced in Grand Canyon include, but are not limited to: climbing cliffs, floating rivers, and traveling in narrow canyons. Nearly everything about a Grand Canyon river trip or hiking trip is dangerous. If you don't want to endanger your life, don't come to Grand Canyon, don't buy this book, and certainly don't use this book.

Nature is constantly changing. Rockslides occur, floods change river and creek channels, beaches erode away, and earthquakes create new canyons altogether. Therefore, any information contained herein should be considered out of date and possibly incorrect.

The author and publisher of *Grand Canyon River Hikes* claims no responsibility for any actions that might be embarked through the use of this book. Any decision that you, the reader, makes to climb, swim, walk, sit, stand, sleep, eat, drink, or breathe is entirely your own. You are burdened with the responsibility to take care of yourself, and any trouble you get into, before or after reading this book, is entirely your problem, and nobody else's. No amount of guidance, either from a guidebook or otherwise, can replace personal judgement.

# Acknowledgments

Assembling a book is a group effort, and this one is no exception. There are many who have assisted this endeavor in one way or another, be it posing for a photo, providing advice and information, offering encouragement, or simply hanging out with me in the Canyon. Thanks to all of you—you know who you are.

A special thanks must go to my cousin Mary. Not only is she the matriarchal funhog of the family that paved the way for my life of adventure years ago, she is also the designer of this book—the one who made it look beautiful. As always, Lisa was an invaluable help as editor, photographer, consultant, hiking partner, and all around cool chick. Thanks to Glenn Rink for some good edits, advice on climbing, and route information. Thanks to Jo Deurbrouck for suggesting that I do "a book on river hikes." Good idea, Jo. My friends at the photography studios were a great help: Dave Edwards, Vivian Lynch, Kate Thompson, Katherine McDonald, and the late Dugald Bremner. I hope you don't disapprove of this too much, Dugz. I have to wonder if you're somewhere writing that "Guidebook to Guidebook Author's Houses" you always joked about. For providing archeological information, I thank Melissa Schroeder from Grand Canyon National Park and the NAU Arch Lab Folks: Lisa Leap, Jennifer Kunde, and Duane Hubbard. I'd go down the river with you guys anytime. And finally, thanks to all the trip leaders that accommodated my frenetic hiking agendas, especially Guus Duijvestijn, R.V. Ward, Elaine Leslie, and Bill Clark.

# Introduction

There are many reasons to go on a river trip through Grand Canyon: legendary rapids, stunning scenery, bonding friendships; but the best thing about a Grand Canyon river trip, for me at least, is the hiking. The river corridor is a spectacular and relaxing place no doubt, but to fully experience the grandeur of the Canyon, one must get away from the beaches, ascend a sinuous side canyon, and gaze across the surreal landscape from some breathtakingly lofty perch.

However, don't expect this guide to lead you to all of those breathtaking places. Most of the routes listed in *Grand Canyon River Hikes* are standards that nearly every river guide has done, some of them many times. These are the obvious places where, with or without a guidebook, most of us would say "let's go check that out." To find the truly spectacular spots you must hike farther, climb higher, and nearly die of thirst once or twice.

I'm selfish, so I have left the relatively "undiscovered" places out of this book, reserved especially for me and my selfish friends. Not that I even know of the truly clandestine places. There are many river guides and backpackers with heaps more experience boating and hiking in Grand Canyon than I. These weathered canyon lovers know that this book barely scratches the surface of Grand Canyon hiking.

Many of these knowledgeable Canyon lovers will not share my enthusiasm for this book. "Why do we want more people traipsing around our canyons?" they'll say. In principle, I have to agree with that sentiment. I certainly prefer not to see others when I am in the wilds. But at the same time that I wish it was all my little secret, I also wish to share my experience with others. I get so much exhilaration, see so much beauty, and feel such goodness in the world when I visit the backcountry that I can only believe these feelings will be experienced by others, too, when they go exploring. I have to think that this is a good thing. Besides, as a human with potentially forty more years on this planet, I want my agenda of personal freedom and unfettered open spaces to be furthered before my four decades are up. A constituency of like-minded individuals helps that cause, and maybe this book will help develop that constituency.

If you are lucky enough to go on a Grand Canyon river trip, I urge you to explore the canyons, ascend the buttes, and trek the trails. Like most good things in life, you'll get out of it what you put into it. When you finally return from your hike, you'll be glad that you went. Be forewarned, acute cases of Canyon fever have been acquired this way. Symptoms include hours of map study, disturbed sleep patterns caused by dreams of brimming slickrock potholes, and an unquenchable desire to find new routes through the Redwall. Good luck in catching it.

## Geology

So much has already been written about Grand Canyon geology that I could hardly have anything more to add to the subject. I do know the major layers, however, and they are shown in the following illustration. There are two acronyms listed here to help you remember the order of the formations. One is the standard academic version and the other is a bit racier. The adult acronym includes Temple Butte Limestone, a difficult to distinguish layer which is found between the Muav and the Redwall.

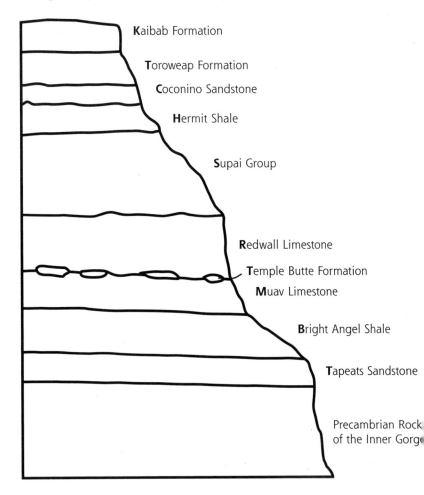

Kaibab Formation

Toroweap Formation

Coconino Sandstone

Hermit Shale

Supai Group

Redwall Limestone

Temple Butte Formation

Muav Limestone

Bright Angel Shale

Tapeats Sandstone

Precambrian Rock of the Inner Gorge

Rock Layers Acronyms

1. **K**now **T**he **C**anyon's **H**istory, **S**tudy **R**ocks **M**ade **B**y **T**ime
2. **K**issing **T**akes **C**oncentration, **H**owever, **S**ome **R**equire **T**itilation by **M**ore **B**reath and **T**ongue

## Hiking in Grand Canyon

Hiking in Grand Canyon presents a unique set of challenges that even experienced trekkers might find difficult. First of all, this is a desert, so water sources are few and far between. Combine this scarcity of water with intense sunshine and crippling heat, and you've got a recipe for dehydration, heat exhaustion, or even deadly heat stroke. In this harsh environment, it doesn't take long for things to turn epic. Be prepared.

If you are planning to walk in the open desert on a hot day my first advice is—don't. Stick to the shady canyon bottoms and creeks when it is hot. If you must go wandering in the stinking hot desert, go in the morning or evening when it is cooler, bring lots of water (and some food too), and wear wet clothing. Before a warm-weather hike in the desert, I always put on a long-sleeved white shirt and shade hat, then jump into the river just before setting out.

Once you do set out, don't expect mindless one-foot-in-front-of-the-other hiking. Grand Canyon is a complex landscape requiring attention. Underfoot is often loose rocks, and your course is often blocked by an imposing ring of cliffs. Finding routes through these cliffs can be a difficult, frustrating, and sometimes dangerous game that usually involves a little climbing. Difficult as it may be, this route-finding game is strangely seductive. It is what captivates dedicated Canyon hikers like Harvey Butchart and those who have followed him.

Before I go any further, I should tell you a little about Harvey Butchart, as you'll hear his name periodically throughout this book. Harvey Butchart is the Wayne Gretzky, Michael Jordan, and Babe Ruth of Grand Canyon hiking. Butchart, a former math professor at Northern Arizona University in Flagstaff, started hiking the Canyon's backcountry in 1945. Over the next four decades, he logged an estimated 12,000 miles of foot travel in Grand Canyon and Marble Gorge. He climbed 83 summits within the Canyon, 25 of which were first-ascents. One of Butchart's greatest accomplishments, in my opinion, is finding 116 different routes to the Colorado River.

The greatest obstacle in his route-finding quest was the Redwall Limestone. It first appears along the river at mile 23 and forms dramatic cliffs all along the Canyon. The Redwall is actually gray rock that has been stained in most places from leaching of the red Hermit and Supai formations above.

At the top of the Supai is the Esplanade, a broad bench of sandstone that offers relatively easy walking across much of the Canyon. Another broad platform good for walking within the Canyon is the Tonto. This is the flat to gently-sloping terrain on the top of the Tapeats Sandstone. On the south side of the river, much of the Tonto Platform is laced with the Tonto Trail, which runs from Hermit Rapid at mile 77 to below Waltenburg at mile 112.

So there you have it, everything you need to know to sound like a Grand Canyon veteran. If you really want to impress your friends around the campfire, just throw together a few of the buzz words from above. It might sound something like this: "Dude, it was gnarly. I got totally fried on the *Tonto*, then I followed this sick *Harvey route* through the *Redwall*. But once I hit the *Esplanade*, it was cruisy."

## Walking softly

Desert is zen. The simple, uncluttered beauty of the desert is not apparent to the casual observer. It is an acquired taste. But once appreciated, a desert's virtues are intensely rewarding. Cliffs sweep in clean unblemished faces, pinnacles of rock teeter on crumbling necks of substrate, and vast spaces are broken only by lonely buttes. Other environments seem cluttered in comparison.

Cryptobiotic soil takes years to form but only seconds to destroy.

Whereas a more busy environment like a forest can hide its wounds, heal its scars, and swallow a man with its canopy, a desert is open, exposed, and vulnerable. Therefore, if we decide to penetrate this harsh and glorious land, we must do it as gently and respectfully as possible. It is essentially impossible to walk cross-country in the desert without affecting the landscape in some way. It is possible, however, to travel with an acceptably low impact in this fragile environment. Stay in streambeds when you can. Floods scour the creekbeds clean periodically, so even your footprints will be wiped away. When not in the creeks, walk on solid rock when possible. You won't leave footprints here, which in turn cause erosion. If there is a trail, use it. It is better to keep our impacts confined rather than making multiple unsightly erosional trails.

Be especially aware of cryptobiotic soil. This is the dark green to black crust of algae, fungus, and lichen that covers much of the desert. Cryptobiotic soil literally holds the dirt together by developing a unifying shield that retains moisture, prevents erosion, and aids in new plant growth. Cryptobiotic soil takes years to form and years to recover once it has been crushed. Avoid it.

I like to think of the desert as one big rock garden, with each arch, rock fin, rock window, cactus, pebble, and boulder placed meticulously in a giant work of art. Take time to investigate this desert microworld of intricate textures and colors and you will find an attention to detail unequaled in the civilized world.

Once you have gained this perspective, walking with care becomes second nature as every footprint is an imperfection, left by you, in this grand masterpiece.

## Archeological sites

Grand Canyon has an estimated 50,000 archeological sites, with nearly 500 located in the river corridor. With such a density of archeologically significant places, it is likely that you will come into contact with one or more sites during your visit to the Canyon. When you do, please follow a few logical guidelines to help keep the site impact-free.

Most ruins are terribly fragile, so don't sit, stand, or lean on any walls of a ruin. These structures have stood for hundreds of years. It would be a shame to let your plump gluteus be the thing that sends them crumbling down. It is not a good idea to eat at a ruin site. Your crumbs will attract rodents who build nests and undermine the stability of the structure. Of course it is illegal to take any artifact or disturb pictographs or petroglyphs. Touching rock art is a disturbance. Your body oils degrade ancient paintings over time. Don't move any artifacts either. We don't need to have all the potsherds in a nice little pile in order to see them. Leave stuff the way you found it.

Basically, archeological sites are open-air museums—treat them as such. Be polite, careful, and aware around any archaeological site you find, and it might still be there when the next generation of river runners pass.

## Native Lands

Native Americans continue to live in and around the Canyon today. We are fortunate to still have these native cultures in the Southwestern U.S. Please respect their customs and property. If you are near a hogan (dome-shaped traditional home of the Navajo), give it a wide berth. It could very well be someone's home, and it is doubtful that they will want to visit with a fleece-wearing stranger who hiked up from the river. If you meet up with a native while hiking on the reservation, greet them modestly and be pre-pared to show them your reservation permit if they ask. **Yes, the reservations have their own permit systems for use of their land.**

Navajo land exists on the east side of the Canyon upstream from the Little Colorado River. Havasupai dwell along Havasu Creek. If you go above Beaver Falls on Havasu Creek, you are on Havasupai lands. All land on river left from mile 165 to mile 273 is the Hualapai reservation.

The traditional home of the Navajo—the hogan.

## Hazards

As our natural areas are increasingly developed, so too are we the people that work and play in these natural places increasingly restrained. When one takes stock of the situation, the trend is disturbing. Cliffs are being closed to climbing, many rivers are off limits to floating, and entire moun-tains are being made inaccessible due to their "invitingly hazardous nature." In today's United States of America, one is no longer free to act within his own parameters of judgment, regardless of how harmless his actions might be. The ultimate loser in this paranoid world of excessive restriction is not the hiker, climber, or kayaker who is arrested for practic-ing his sport. The real loser is freedom itself.

In the current climate of non-individual-responsibility, land use managers have lost sight of the basic natural laws that govern our planet such as gravity, life, and death. Over-trained to "manage" the land and its inhabitants with "mediation tactics" and "preventative measures," these involuntary despots can no longer recall what it is they are trying to prevent, or who it is, exactly, that they are trying to mediate. Yet still, they forge ahead in their paranoid confusion, making new rules and more paperwork, all the while suppressing our freedoms.

With the misconception that it is their duty to protect us from ourselves stamped on their conformist brains, even childishly simple signs like "caution—cliff edge" are no longer enough. There was a time when it was clear that humans inherently understood gravity, but apparently that enlightened age has passed us by. Now, regulatory agencies feel they must erect railings, gates, fences, barricades, signs, and walls to manage human traffic and keep people away from the edge, out of harm's way.

> **"A venturesome minority will always be eager to set off on their own, and no obstacles should be placed in their path; let them take risks, for Godsake, let them get lost, sunburnt, stranded, drowned, eaten by bears, buried alive under avalanches—that is the right and privilege of any free American."**
> —*Edward Abbey*

The entities that construct these eyesores on the landscape have the audacity to proclaim resource protection as the motivation behind their actions. The irony in this, however, is even too much for the bureaucrats to miss. Therefore, their second line of defense in explaining closures is reverently referred to as "saving lives," as if they have some moral responsibility to save our lives.

This so-called moral responsibility to save other people's lives has the ring of righteousness, but it is in fact the ultimate oppression. What could be more oppressive than one exerting his own power in order to control another's fate? The purest freedom, the ultimate human right, is to determine one's own destiny. For an outside party to influence that destiny and then take the moral high ground in defense of their infringement is not only a crime against the individual. It is a crime against the natural order, against life itself.

But in a practical sense, it is pointless to discuss the inequities of this so-called moral responsibility, because the proclamation of moral responsibility is a lie anyway. The real issue behind the closures, laws, and other obscene ordinances we taxpayers must now face is money; money that is controlled by a complex web of insurance companies, attorneys, and business. The insurance companies have the money, business makes the money, and the attorneys (along with their greedy, unethical clients) tirelessly try to take the money.

Given this list of power brokers who control the money, and subsequently our freedom, it is easy to finger the attorneys as the scapegoats. But before we "start by killing all the lawyers," as Shakespeare wrote, consider that attorneys don't bring lawsuits by themselves. There is always a "victim" trying to strike it rich at the core of any dispute. Also consider that attorneys don't make decisions in a court of law, judges and juries do. These are the esteemed entities that unwittingly tip the first domino in the wave of regulation that shackles our freedoms.

Until the American legal system is changed, making it less desirable to bring lawsuits against common sense, we are burdened with an uphill battle. For the time being, the only way to level the playing field is to enter the playing field. (Lawyers that hike, climb, or boat, are you listening?) Once legal precedents are established reaffirming personal responsibility as the law of the land, the profit will be taken out of frivolous claims brought with dollar signs in the eyes. And when the profit disappears, so will the money-mining insurance companies, lawyers, and plaintiffs magically return to the dark crevices from which they came.

The natural world is ever shrinking from development—to let it shrink due to bureaucracy as well is tragic. As outdoor enthusiasts, we must challenge all closures, rules, and restrictions designed to save us from ourselves, and as proponents of freedom, we must firmly grasp our right to make our own decisions, to control our own fate, to simply be.

## Be Safe

Once we regain the right to take care of ourselves, we should hold up our end of the bargain and take care of ourselves. Rescues are expensive. Most of us would no sooner give our tax dollars to an autocratic bureaucrat than to an irresponsible hiker in need of rescue. So then, be prepared. The challenge and independence of being beyond the safety net of immediate rescue is refreshing. Embrace it.

Anything from an appendicitis to a sprained ankle could present a life threatening situation in the wilds. Don't be surprised when a medical emergency sprouts up in the outback. Basic first aid skills are a must for a canyon hiker. There are many good first aid courses available now that are specifically geared toward the wilderness setting. Taking one of these courses is a good first step in preparing yourself for Grand Canyon hiking.

A first aid kit should be carried when hiking away from the river. That giant first aid kit that you showed the ranger at the put in does no good if it is on the raft and the injured party is two miles up a side canyon. Most injuries on river trips occur away from the river, so it makes sense for your first aid kit to make it away from the river, too. It's not practical to take a bulky bunch of medical supplies hiking with you, but a small first aid kit per group is essential.

"Just another victim of the things he has done."
—Neil Peart

I recommend buying one of the pre-assembled backcountry kits on the market. They are compact, logically organized, and easier than trying to assemble your own first aid kit from the local drug store. Adventure Medical Kits are the best I've found. They were designed by a doctor who is a boater and experienced backcountry traveler, so they contain all the practical items for a wilderness setting.

The best way to receive a rattlesnake bite is to step on or pick up a rattlesnake.

Ken Abbott

## Flash Floods

It is easy to get complacent about flash floods because they are so rare, but when they do strike, it is with "great vengeance and furious anger," as Samuel L. Jackson might quote. Consider the following scene:

You are standing in the bottom of a narrow sheer-walled gorge when a rumbling sound from upstream is heard. Seconds later a moving wall of mud, sticks, rocks, and scummy foam comes barreling towards you like a runaway train. If you are lucky, you grab a protruding rock shelf as the wave hits, and you are able to stay out of the main current by clutching the rock until the floodwaters recede.

More probable, though, is the scenario in which you are pounded in the back by what feels like an angry linebacker on a blindside blitz. You can't breathe, but even more frightening than that is the beating you are taking from the walls, boulders, and logs that pummel you indiscriminately. Maybe you are fortunate enough to get struck with such force that you go unconscious, never to awaken to this horrifying scene. If you are not this fortunate, however, you struggle to the surface and get a desperate breath of air before being prematurely jerked back under the maelstrom, unintentionally sucking in a mouthful of the gritty scum on your way down. This routine may repeat itself several more times until finally all goes black, and your limp body slams along the bottom of the newly-formed river before coming to rest in a strainer of logs or a debris-filled pool.

Flash floods are tremendously rare because they only form after a severe, torrential rainfall. However, it just so happens that torrential rains occasionally fall in Grand Canyon. When this hard rain falls on the rocky, non-absorptive desert, walls of water develop.

Due to the surface tension of water, it can collect upstream faster than the leading edge of the runoff can move. Combine this with a narrow canyon, where the nose of the flood gets compressed and has nowhere to go but up, and you've got the often mentioned, rarely seen "wall of water."

Heavy rain most commonly occurs in July, August, and September in Grand Canyon. During these months, be especially wary of the weather. It does not have to rain directly on you for you to be caught in a flash flood; it merely has to rain somewhere in your drainage basin. The bigger the drainage basin and narrower the canyon, the greater the flash flood risk.

# How To Use This Book

### River Mile
Assuming Lees Ferry is mile 0, Diamond Creek is mile 226, and Pearce Ferry is mile 280, this is the point at which the start of the hike is located—in river miles. These mileages correlate directly with Larry Stevens' *The Colorado River in Grand Canyon—A Guide.*

### Creek Right and Left
Most of you already know what it means when someone says river right. But just for the record, here is an explanation: River right means the right side of the river as you are looking downstream. So then, if you are looking upstream, river right would be on your left.

By following the convention of river right and left, we establish a common reference point, which helps eliminate confusion. Remember, though, the direction must be preceded by river or creek for the convention to be in use. "The butte is on the left" is only a useful statement if your relative location is firmly established. However, by stating "The butte is on creek left," we know that it is on the left if you are looking downstream.

### Time
This is the average time it would take a 6-person group to enjoy the hike, stopping to space out a little and look at a few lizards. Time spent rum-

maging through drybags for hiking shoes, putting on sunscreen, and adjusting attitudes before the hike is not taken into account. Remember that an average is just that. A group of fit river guides will only take half as much time as I've listed, whereas people unfamiliar with hiking on the uneven, rugged terrain of Grand Canyon will probably take longer than the indicated time estimate.

## Difficulty

Difficult—the very word is subjective. To give a completely accurate and objective assessment of the difficulty of any rapid, climb, or hike is impossible. How can one accurately describe a route by simply using adjectives like challenging, hard, and harder? One can't. Just ask the British, who in the past used the phrase "very severe" to define a level of climbing difficulty. When the "very severe" climbs became commonplace, a new category was established called "extremely severe." Next came "exceptionally severe." Thankfully the system was abandoned before they got to "really totally super-duper severe." Clearly, words alone can't accurately convey difficulty.

This "how hard is it?" dilemma gave birth to the world of rating systems. Mountain climbers were the first to rate their routes, developing a numerical frame of reference from one to six. Level one was basic hiking, and level six was difficult climbing requiring artificial aid to ascend. This scale is still in use, and has served as the building block for other, much more complex rating systems.

In the 1950s, climbers expanded the fifth class of this system by adding decimal points. This was intended to more specifically convey the difficulty of selected climbing routes. Originally 5.0 to 5.9 was established, but as more difficult climbs were done, the scale expanded to 5.10, then 5.11. This trend continues, and today the hardest climbing in the world is rated 5.15.

Unfortunately, over time climbers have disregarded the lower end of 5th class, making it essentially obsolete. It is nearly impossible to find ratings under 5.4 anymore. Some guidebooks now lump together anything judged to be easier than 5.4 as "easy 5th class."

In the interest of giving the most accurate information possible about the canyoneering routes listed in this book, I have used ratings in the lower 5th class. My hope is that hikers who can manage 5.0, but feel uncomfortable with 5.4 will be better informed when they embark on a hike.

The following analogy is a gross generalization that most rock climbers will be aghast at reading. But since the systems in place offer little help to beginning climbers, I will attempt to elucidate the issue with a household analogy. After all, I could hardly make the rating game more confusing at this point.

For climbing neophytes, perhaps the lower end of fifth class climbing can be explained as such: A climb to the top of a vertical 30-foot extension ladder would roughly equate to a 5.0 climb. Take away one out of two rungs on the ladder and you have an increase in difficulty to a 5.1 climb.

Of those remaining rungs, saw them in half and now it is a 5.2 climb. As you can see, with every decimal point the handholds get fewer and smaller. It is generally thought that nothing beyond 5.9 can be climbed without the use of specialized rubber climbing shoes. A climb of 5.14 is pretty much miraculous.

Going in the other direction, if our ladder were lowered from the vertical to 60 degrees, the climbing would be reduced to 4th class. Make the rungs fatter and reduce the angle even more so that fearless people with good balance can walk up the ladder without the use of their hands, and it is now 3rd class. The amount of exposure (how far you will fall) plays into the rating game as well, complicating the issue even more.

Of course these are generalizations. Actually, it is difficult to even find a ladder most of the time in Grand Canyon, especially when you really need one. But I hope these examples help you get an idea of what it means when the book says: "the route around the pool is 5.1 with 20 feet of exposure." It means you should've brought your ladder.

In a more general sense, the categories **Easy**, **Moderate**, and **Difficult** are listed to explain the relative difficulty of the hike. The key word here is relative. An "easy" hike is only easy compared to the other hikes in this book. The same is true of moderate and difficult routes. Additionally, there will often be a sentence or two under the difficulty heading explaining why the hike is so damn difficult.

### Wet or Dry?

A wet hike is one in which water will play a major role. In some cases, the canyon bottom will be flooded from wall to wall. Other times, there is just enough water along the route so that it is easier to wade through it than to try and keep your feet dry. Sturdy river sandals work well on wet hikes, though canyoneering shoes offer more protection. Teva offers a wide range of footwear suitable for wet hikes..

Dry hikes are suitable for sturdy dry hiking boots. There might be some water along a dry hike, but it is minimal enough so that you will be able to keep your feet dry without too much fancy footwork.

### Ideal Weather

Under the Ideal Weather listing, you will find one or more of the following four categories: Cool, Moderate, Hot, or Any. Remember that this is only the ideal weather for the route. You could probably do a hike listed as cool in moderate weather, but doing a cool hike in hot weather will be miserable—if not suicidal. Every experienced Canyon hiker has at least one story of an epic dehydration/heat exhaustion death march. Others never got to tell their story. Be careful.

Following is what the terms cool, moderate, and hot mean in this book. All temperatures are in Fahrenheit.

A **Cool** day means temperatures are less than 70 degrees if it is sunny, or less than 80 degrees if it is cloudy. On cool days, you will be wearing splash gear and trying to stay dry while on the river. Most people will be seeking the warmth of the sun, and those sinister black rocks of the inner gorge hold welcome heat, if any at all. Cool days are usually found between October and April.

On **Moderate** days the afternoon temperatures range from 70 to 90 degrees. A sunny 75 degree day would be considered moderate, as would a rainy day in the 80s. Warm rainy days like this sometimes occur during the summer thunderstorm season. On a sunny moderate day, most will seek shade by afternoon, but the heat isn't stifling. It will be a little too warm for open steep hikes like Vulcan's Throne, but not quite hot enough to really appreciate the shade and water of wet canyon hikes like Elves Chasm.

A **Hot** day is the norm from June through August in the bottom of Grand Canyon, although a strong "monsoon" flow in July and August can sometimes bring welcome clouds or rain. Temperatures on a hot day are in the 90s or 100s. Most human activity is geared around shade and water on these days. On or in the water is the best place to be, and long hikes in the open desert are out of the question.

If **Any** is listed under Ideal Weather, the route is suitable in just about any weather conditions. Typically, a route listed as Any is a shady but dry canyon bottom.

## Potential
The Potential category is intended to give you an idea of the different hiking options for a given area. Often, the standard hike that I've described is just the tip of the iceberg, and enthusiastic hikers will want to keep going beyond the described route. For them, there is the Potential category. This is where they can find out if a canyon "goes" or not.

## Camp
This category provides information on camps that are at or near the described hike. By no means do you have to camp at the locations that are mentioned here. There are many fine camps in Grand Canyon that rarely get used. Break from the mold and camp somewhere different—you'll like it.

Backpackers occasionally use the same camps as river runners. Realize that backpackers have hiked many strenuous miles to reach that secluded beach. A beer-swilling river party is probably the last thing they expect or want to see. If you wind up at the same camp with backpackers, be courteous. Offer them cold drinks and fresh food, and you'll likely get along just fine.

## Maps
Simplicity, rather than detail, was the primary goal in the creation of the maps of this book. Don't expect to find every terrain feature you see on your hike to be shown on the map. For that kind of detail, a topographic map is needed. However, by reading the route description and following the map, you should have little trouble in staying found.

Here are a few helpful hints about the maps: Only the most significant canyon rims are shown. River mile is indicated as R.M. These mileages correlate with the Stevens river guide. The maps are oriented with respect to the river, which is running from left to right through the entire book. To find where north is, look for the big N, usually near the top of the map. Scale Is displayed as a black line below the map indicating a quarter of a mile. When looking at the scale, remember that map miles are generally shorter than actual on-the-ground miles.

Though a topographical map is really the best type to have, I hope that the simple map sketches in this book will help.

# The Hikes

# Spencer Trail

**River Mile:** -0.7—right
**Time:** 3 hours
**Difficulty:** Moderate. This route is all uphill and on somewhat loose rock, but there is no climbing involved.
**Wet or Dry?:** Dry
**Ideal Weather:** Cool
**Potential:** At the top of the Spencer Trail you are on the Paria Plateau—an intriguing desert of sand dunes and slickrock waiting for exploration.
**Camp:** Lees Ferry

**Route Description:** The Spencer Trail is a cairned route which leads to the top of the cliffs just north of Lees Ferry. The views from the top are spectacular. Hiking up the Spencer Trail is a great way to loosen up those hiking legs in preparation for the long river journey ahead.

From the boat ramp at Lees Ferry, walk upstream through the parking lot and onto the river trail. About 400 yards from the ramp, there is a cairn on the uphill side of the river trail indicating the start of the Spencer Trail. If you pass the submerged steamer, you've gone about 30 yards too far.

The route zigzags its way uphill with cairns marking the way. Pay attention and keep your eyes peeled here; the route is easy to lose in a couple of places. The exposure on this route is minimal, so even acrophobiacs should have little trouble in reaching the stupendous views at the top.

To the north, Lake Powell, the Kaiparowits Plateau, and Navajo Mountain fill the horizon. In the foreground, the Colorado placidly twists through the depths of Glen Canyon.

To the south, the Paria River and Lees Ferry are in view. The Vermillion Cliffs and Lees Backbone frame the scene, as Marble Gorge snakes its way toward the Kaibab Plateau.

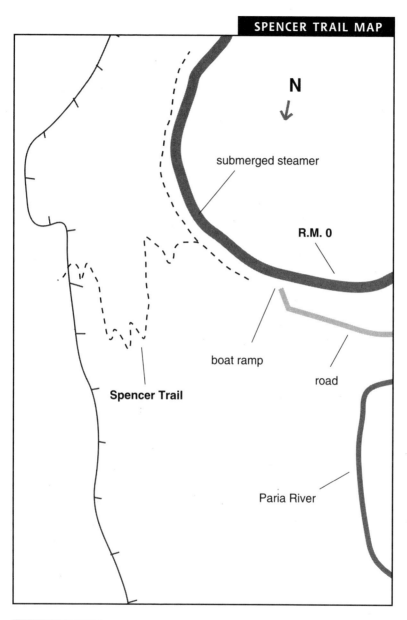

## SPENCER TRAIL MAP

N

submerged steamer

**R.M. 0**

boat ramp

road

**Spencer Trail**

Paria River

1/4 mile

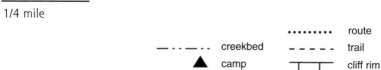

........ route

— ·· — ·· creekbed        − − − − trail

▲ camp        ⊤ ⊤ ⊤ cliff rim

Viewing the Great American Desert

# Cathedral Wash

**River Mile:** 2.8—right
**Time:** 1.5 hours to the road and back
**Difficulty:** Easy to Moderate. It is all simple hiking except for one 4-foot ledge that must be scrambled up.
**Wet or Dry?:** Dry
**Ideal Weather**: Cool or Moderate
**Potential:** Upstream from the Lees Ferry road, Cathedral Wash leads to the base of the Vermillion Cliffs two miles away.
**Camp:** There is no substantial camp here and it's illegal for river trips to camp above Navajo Bridge.

**Route Description:** Relieved and elated to finally be riding the powerful spine of the Colorado, most boaters will be reluctant to stop only 3 miles from the put-in. Nonetheless, Cathedral Wash is a wonderful little canyon that is worthy of exploration. If you aren't able to pull yourself away from the river on day one, try sneaking away on the day before your put-in for a hike here. The upper end of Cathedral Wash is 4 miles down the road from Lees Ferry.

Cathedral Wash is short and scenic. From the river, only 10 minutes of walking up the well-trodden creekbed will have you in beautiful Kaibab Limestone narrows. There are a few falls in the canyon, but easy routes along flat shelves of rock lead around them all.

When powerlines cross the canyon, you are about two thirds of the way to the road. A sign indicating the park boundary is located in the upper end of Cathedral, just downstream from a fork. Either fork leads out to the open desert and the Lees Ferry road, but the north fork is shorter. If you have no interest in encountering pavement on your river trip, turn around at the park sign.

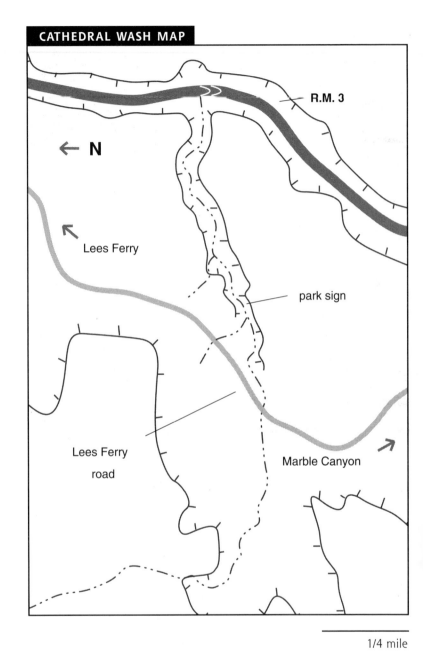

# CATHEDRAL WASH MAP

R.M. 3

← N

Lees Ferry

park sign

Lees Ferry road

Marble Canyon

1/4 mile

......... route

– – – – trail    –·–·– creekbed

╤╤ cliff rim    ▲ camp

Limestone narrows in Cathedral Wash

# Jackass Creek

**River Mile:** 8—left
**Time:** 1 hour, 20 minutes to the narrows and back
**Difficulty:** Moderate. There is some scrambling here and a 5th class climb is needed to go beyond the falls.
**Wet or Dry?**: Dry
**Ideal Weather**: Moderate or Cool
**Potential:** Two hours upstream is the open desert above Marble Gorge, and highway 89A.
**Camp:** There are big camps on both sides of the river here.

**Route Description:** Jackass Creek is a popular route among local fisherman for getting to the blue-ribbon trout of the Colorado River. Because of this, unfortunately, the canyon has suffered some wounds. Every step of the route up the canyon has been spray-painted with fluorescent green directional arrows, and various types of trash linger in the rocks of the creekbed. Despite all this, a Jackass Creek hike is still worthwhile, offering narrow scenery and fun scrambling through giant boulders.

Huge boulders fill the canyon bottom in the lower end of Jackass, and the progress is relatively slow as you wind in and out of the fallen rocks. Upstream, the canyon walls close in and the canyon's character changes from an open debris-filled bed to a narrow draw of bedrock slides. Not long after entering the narrow part of the canyon, a fall of 30 feet signals a good turnaround spot. A 5.0 climb will get you beyond this fall and into the upper canyon, which soon dissipates into the open desert at the foot of the Echo Cliffs. Don't proceed above the fall without a hiking permit from the Navajo Reservation.

Jackass Creek is probably named after the many burros that once roamed throughout Grand Canyon. Miners brought the animals to the Canyon in the late 1800s and they soon thrived here (the burros, not the miners). As the decades passed, burros increasingly competed with the native bighorn sheep for resources. This led the park service to eventually remove the burros from the Canyon.

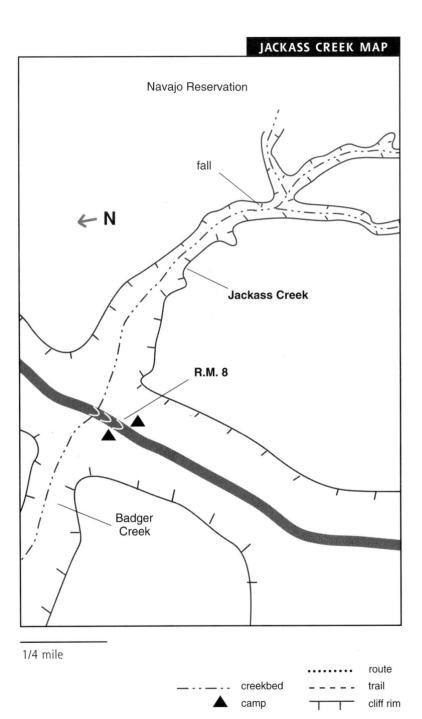

Navajo Reservation

fall

← N

Jackass Creek

R.M. 8

Badger
Creek

1/4 mile

········· route
—··—·· creekbed     — — — — trail
▲ camp     ⊤——⊤ cliff rim

Jackass Creek is a popular route among fishermen.

# Soap Creek

**River Mile:** 11.2—right
**Time:** 45 minutes is enough time for a nice stroll up the canyon.
**Difficulty:** Moderate. There is lots of boulder hopping and a scramble or two.
**Wet or Dry?**: Dry, though there are occasional pools.
**Ideal Weather:** Cool or Moderate
**Potential:** A 2 or 3 hour hike will have you out of the canyon near the community of Cliff Dwellers.
**Camp:** Two big camps are located here. One is upstream of the rapid and one is downstream. Both are on river right.

**Route Description:** Soap Creek is a popular first night's camp. Despite this, few river runners hike here. The hike up Soap is not spectacular, but it is a nice place to get away from camp and the roar of the river.

The best scenery is near the mouth of the canyon. You'll be boulder hopping and scrambling around small falls in the creekbed—typical Grand Canyon hiking. A 15 minute walk from camp is sufficient to get you into the quiet solitude of Marble Gorge. However, ambitious hikers can make it out Soap Creek to the rim of the Canyon. If you decide to go for the rim, you will take a cairned route on creek right around the biggest fall. At the major fork high in the canyon, head straight, avoiding the canyon that branches north. At the top, there is a B.L.M. trailhead near highway 89A.

Soap Creek was named when explorer Jacob Hamblin boiled badger here in a kettle of alkaline water. In the morning, he was left with a kettle of soap resulting from the combination of the badger's fats and the alkaline water.

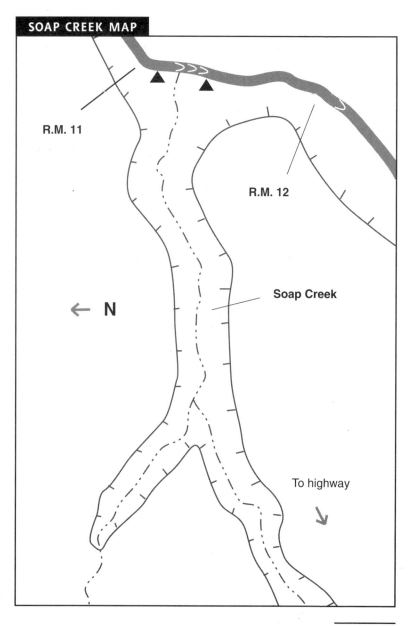

**SOAP CREEK MAP**

R.M. 11

← N

R.M. 12

Soap Creek

To highway

1/4 mile

·········· route

– – – – – trail

⊤ ⊤ cliff rim

▲ camp

– · – · – · creekbed

In the Big Ditch at last

# Rider Canyon

**River Mile:** 16.8—right
**Time:** One hour round-trip to the first major climb
**Difficulty:** Moderate. A 5.1 climb is necessary to get by a fall 0.5 miles from the river.
**Wet or Dry?:** Dry. Though there are some pools, most in the lower 0.5 miles can be easily avoided.
**Ideal Weather:** Any weather is fine unless you plan to go beyond the falls, then you'll want it cool.
**Potential:** A route to the rim is located two miles up the canyon. To get to the rim and back will take 6 to 8 hours.
**Camp:** A medium-sized camp is located at the mouth of Rider. However, this camp is directly below House Rock Rapid, so some boats might have trouble catching the eddy.

**Route Description:** Rider Canyon is overlooked by most river runners because it is located at House Rock Rapid, the toughest rapid on the river thus far. Those who do make the stop will be rewarded with an off-the-beaten-path side canyon. Rider is just an average place by Grand Canyon standards, but it would be considered extraordinary were it anywhere else.

For hiking in Rider, boat parking is best done above House Rock Rapid on the right. There is a large surging eddy and sandy beach below the drop, but this eddy is hard to catch for large rafts, especially if you blow the run.

The lower end of Rider is a somewhat narrow canyon in the Supai Group. There are usually a few muddy pools in the creekbed, but with a little scrambling they can be avoided. About 0.5 miles up from the river, a water-filled narrows below a chokestone marks the end of the hike for most people.

For climbers, there is a 5.1 climb on creek left that avoids the narrows and the pool. Once above this climb, the canyon opens more, though there are still a few scattered pools. There is a cairned route to the rim about 2 miles from the river, on creek right. It goes through some large broken chunks of Kaibab Limestone near the rim. At the top of this route, you'll find yourself in the vacant House Rock Valley, with views of the Vermillion Cliffs and Kaibab Plateau.

The route out of Rider Canyon was used in one of Grand Canyon's first wilderness rescues of modern times. In 1890, the Robert Stanton expedition had trouble when Frederick Nims (the photographer for the trip) fell and was badly injured. Stanton hiked out of Rider Canyon and trudged 35 miles back to Lees Ferry for help. In the meantime, the rest of the party rigged a stretcher for Nims and carried him to the rim of the canyon, where they endured a cold snowy night waiting for the arrival of a wagon from Lees Ferry. The next day, Nims was transported back to Lees Ferry where he remained for a week before getting a ride to Winslow, Arizona and the nearest doctor.

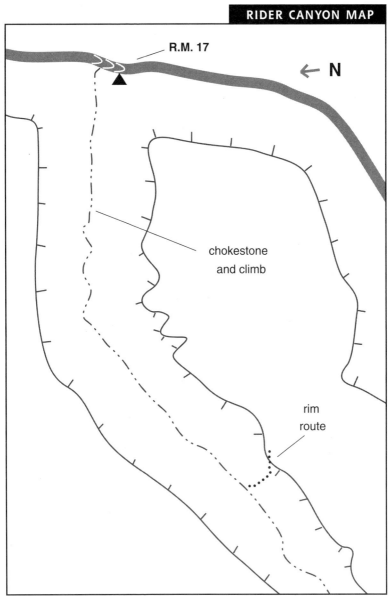

RIDER CANYON MAP

R.M. 17

← N

chokestone
and climb

rim
route

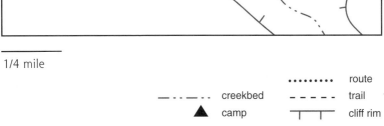

1/4 mile

········ route

—··—··— creekbed     − − − − trail

▲ camp     ⊤⊤⊤⊤ cliff rim

Backpacking in Rider Canyon

# North Canyon

**River Mile:** 20.5—right
**Time:** 1 hour, 20 minutes
**Difficulty:** Easy to Moderate.
**Wet or Dry?:** Dry, but some will want to wade across the first major pool and explore the narrows.
**Ideal Weather:** Moderate or Hot
**Potential:** A fall stops progress 0.6 miles from the river. There is a climber's route here that leads to the Esplanade. The route is on creek left just upstream from the initial pool.
**Camp:** There are camps both above and below the mouth of North. Both camps are on the right.

**Route Description:** North Canyon is the first really "classic" hike encountered along the river. Polished Supai narrows and gorgeous reflective pools reward hikers that make the hike upstream.

The route up North Canyon is mostly up the ledges and boulders of the creekbed. There are a couple of scrambles that make this hike challenging for some and merely interesting for others. At the major fall 0.3 miles from the river, look for a trail leading up to the right (creek left). This short trail will lead you around the fall and back into the creek bottom.

You'll know you are approaching the end when you encounter a beautiful lone willow tree in the narrowing canyon. Just upstream from the willow, there is a canyon-wide pool backed by a trickling water slide. Most will be content to end their hike here, but the adventurous might wish to wade across the pool and scramble into the narrows upstream.

With a little climbing, you can explore for about 200 more yards before reaching a vertical 40-foot fall that would stop even Spiderman. If the creek is running at just the right level, there are some fun waterslides connecting the pools in the narrows.

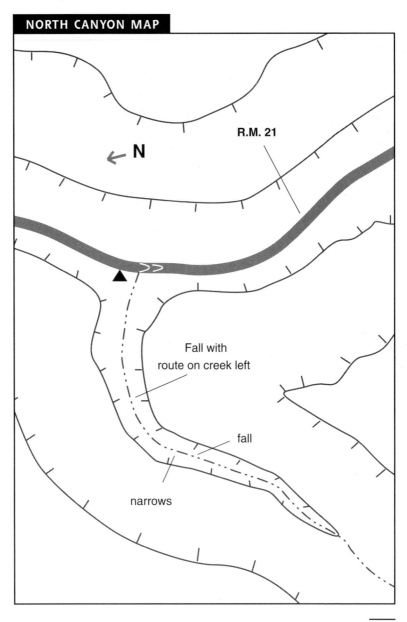

R.M. 21

← N

Fall with
route on creek left

fall

narrows

1/4 mile

.......... route

- - - - - trail    —··—·· creekbed

⊤⊤⊤ cliff rim    ▲ camp

A river trip walks up the bed of North Canyon.

# Silver Grotto

**River Mile:** 29.1—left
**Time:** 1 hour
**Difficulty:** Difficult. Swimming and climbing is required to explore here.
**Wet or Dry?:** Wet
**Ideal Weather:** Hot
**Potential:** A fall stops even gnarly climbers at 0.3 miles.
**Camp:** There is a medium-sized camp at the mouth of Silver Grotto.

**Route Description:** This short hike offers some of the best narrow canyon scenery in the entire Grand Canyon. Silver Grotto is a must-see for anyone with a fascination for wet and narrow canyons. Polished limestone walls twist upward, and giant bathtubs of cold rainwater fill the canyon floor. Upstream travel here is slow and difficult, but also interesting and exciting.

To get into the canyon, follow the faint path that leads to a short climb (5.0 10') on the creek right side of the wash. From the top of this initial climb, it is an easy 40-yard walk to the mouth of the enchanting Silver Grotto narrows. To proceed upstream farther requires lots of swimming and climbing.

The first move is a down-run on smooth sloping limestone into the canyon bottom. Most parties set a rope here for the return route. Next comes the first swim. Or, if you like a challenge, try the friction walk around the creek left side of the pool. A short scramble up a waterslide will have you at the next pool, where a momentum critical circle-run across the wall might keep you out of the water for the time being.

From here, it is once again swimming and slithering to attain upstream. For climbers, there is a 5.7 route on creek right that provides a challenge. If you peel, you'll wind up sliding ten feet into a pool. Though a sprained or broken ankle is possible with a fall here, I found it to be a thankfully soft landing.

One more 4th class scramble gets you to an open amphitheater backed by another pool and a 20' slide—the end of the line.

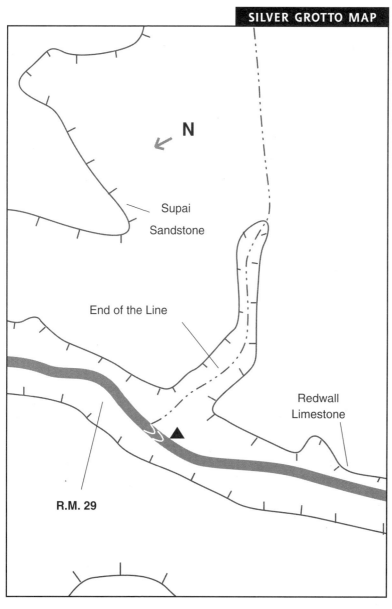

N

Supai
Sandstone

End of the Line

Redwall
Limestone

R.M. 29

1/4 mile

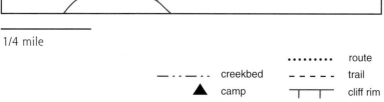

·········· route

—··—··· creekbed     — — — — trail

▲ camp     ⊤⊤ cliff rim

Typical Silver Grotto hiking

# South Canyon

**River Mile:** 31.5—right
**Time:** 15 minutes
**Difficulty:** Easy in the lower end. It is difficult to go through the Redwall and beyond.
**Wet or Dry?:** Dry. However, sometimes floods gouge the gravel from the creekbed, creating pools.
**Ideal Weather:** Any for the lower narrows. Cool or moderate weather is best for exploration above the Redwall.
**Potential:** There are routes to the rim up both South Canyon and Bedrock Canyon—a major tributary. Getting to the rim via either of these canyons is an all-day venture taking 6 to 10 hours one way.
**Camp:** There are two camps here. One is above the drainage, and the bigger camp is below. Backpackers often occupy a third camp at the mouth of the canyon.

**Route Description:** South Canyon has nice Redwall narrows near its confluence with the Colorado that make for a nice, short hike. If you're looking for a full-day hike, some 5th class bouldering will gain access to a wealth of hiking options above the Redwall. There is also a trail upstream from the mouth of South that leads up through the Redwall.

The Redwall narrows at the lower end of South Canyon are "lovely, dark and deep," as Robert Frost might say. A gravel riverbed makes for relatively easy walking except when chokestones cause a hindrance. These chokestone boulders get progressively bigger, and climbing them becomes more difficult as you travel upstream. One climb is often aided with the use of a log. This spot is about a 5 minute walk from the river and a good turnaround point unless you're determined to climb, scramble and boulder hop a long way.

Once above the Redwall, the canyon opens and boulder hopping gets you through the lower Supai layers. At the junction of a major side canyon in the lower Supai, a cairned route leads up the creek right slope and along ledges, bypassing a fall. Shortly above this fall, after the cairned route re-joins the creekbed, you'll reach the junction of South and Bedrock Canyons.

In Bedrock Canyon, you'll find playful Supai narrows before reaching two falls with 5th class climbs around them. Our party made it through the Coconino Sandstone and saw a route through the Kaibab Limestone to the rim. I haven't been up South Canyon beyond the Bedrock confluence, but there are routes to the rim here, too.

Backpackers reach the river at South Canyon by using a trail that traverses the top of the Redwall. This trail leads away from the river at the upper South camp—about 200 yards upstream from the mouth of the canyon.

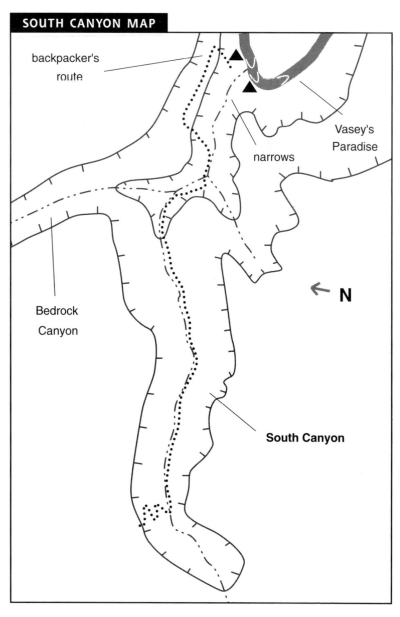

# SOUTH CANYON MAP

backpacker's
route

narrows

Vasey's
Paradise

Bedrock
Canyon

← N

South Canyon

1/4 mile

·········  route
‑ ‑ ‑ ‑ ‑  trail          ‑ · ‑ · ‑ ·  creekbed
┬─┬─  cliff rim    ▲  camp

Above South Canyon

# Nautiloid Canyon

**River Mile:** 34.8—left
**Time:** 30 minutes
**Difficulty:** Easy to Moderate. This is a very short hike, but a 4th class climb is necessary to enter the canyon.
**Wet or Dry?:** Dry
**Ideal Weather:** Any
**Potential:** A fall stops progress 200 yards from the river.
**Camp:** There is a small camp at Nautiloid.

**Route Description:** Nautiloids are ancient deep-sea creatures that propelled themselves by pumping water through their bodies. Here in Nautiloid Canyon you can see the fossilized remains of these strange beings.

There are several ways to scramble into the canyon, but the easiest way is a 4th class route up some sharp limestone on the upstream (creek right) side of the canyon.

Once in the canyon bottom, look for the ribbed fish outlines in the gray limestone underfoot. A bucket of water is nice to have on hand to view the fossils. When the fossils are wet, the bedrock comes alive in an ocean of ancient sea life. Besides the nautiloids, there are fossilized crinoid stems—the little cheerio circles imbedded in the rock.

Even if you're not into the paleontology of Nautiloid Canyon, it still makes a nice stop. It is similar to Silver Grotto, though not as dramatic. The canyon is a quiet, shady place with a huge limestone dryfall at the back.

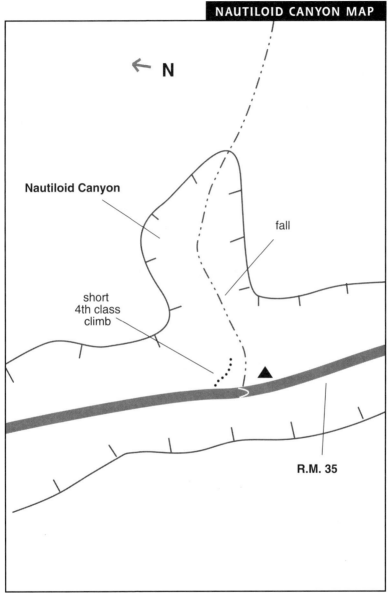

← N

Nautiloid Canyon

fall

short
4th class
climb

R.M. 35

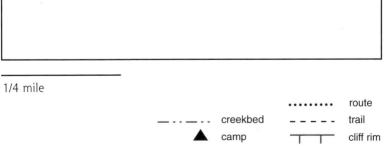

1/4 mile

·········  route

—··—··—  creekbed  — — — —  trail

▲  camp  |‾|‾|‾|  cliff rim

"Wow! Look at those nautiloids."

# Buck Farm Canyon

**River Mile:** 41.0—right
**Time:** To go to the Muav narrows 0.7 miles up and return it will take 45 minutes.
**Difficulty:** Moderate
**Wet or Dry?:** Dry. Though there is some water in the canyon, the footing is mostly dry.
**Ideal Weather:** Any
**Potential:** A Redwall fall blocks progress at 1.5 miles.
**Camp:** There is a nice medium-large camp at the mouth of the canyon.

**Route Description:** Buck Farm Canyon is home to giant Redwall faces and trickling springs supporting colonies of ferns. It is a good place to find soothing greenery and moisture on a hot day.

From the mouth of the canyon, you will be boulder hopping up a steep and dry creekbed until outcrops of Muav begin to bring more interesting scenery and seeps of water to the scene. When large boulders that force you to climb block the creek bottom, look for easier routes up ledges of limestone on creek right.

When you reach a big cottonwood tree in the canyon nearly a mile from the river, you have two options: Either proceed straight ahead into some Muav narrows backed by a chokestone, or continue exploring upstream via a route on creek left.

Just beyond the cottonwood tree are the nicest narrows of this canyon. The gray rock walls are decorated with delicate ferns that drip clear water onto the wet sand underfoot. It is a peaceful and air-conditioned place.

If you decide to go upstream of the narrows, use a route that leads up a rockslide on creek left at the cottonwood tree. Though this route is easy to follow as it traverses back into the creekbed, there is a little exposure along the way. Once back in the creekbed, it is only a few hundred yards farther to a fall in the Redwall that will turn all but good climbers back.

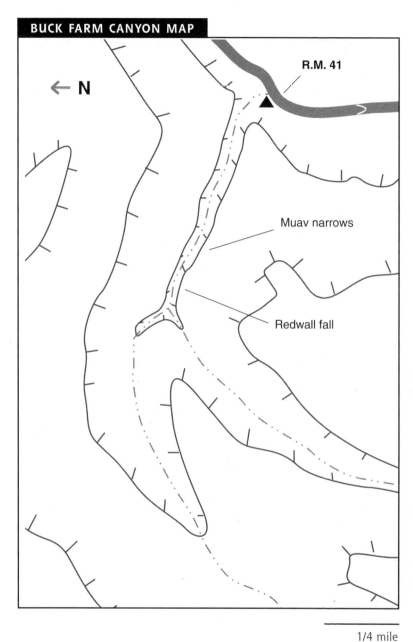

## BUCK FARM CANYON MAP

← N

R.M. 41

Muav narrows

Redwall fall

1/4 mile

•••••••• route
– – – – – trail          –··–··– creekbed
⊤⊤⊤⊤ cliff rim      ▲ camp

44

Enjoying Buck Farm Canyon

# Eminence Break

**River Mile:** 44.4—left
**Time:** 7 or 8 hours round trip to the rim. 1 hour round-trip to the top of the Redwall.
**Difficulty:** Difficult to hike up the Eminence Break to the rim. Moderate to go to the top of the Redwall.
**Wet or Dry?:** Dry
**Ideal Weather:** Cool
**Potential:** This route leads to the rim. What more could you want?
**Camp:** You can access this route from the President Harding Camp just upstream. There is also a camp directly at the trailhead.

**Route Description:** Eminence Break is a prominent fault that runs across many miles of desert before plunging into Marble Gorge. This noticeable route from river to rim has been used by humans for several hundred years. Walking in the ancient's footsteps along this natural passageway makes a great layover day hike to the rim.

The route begins as a steep but easy-to-follow trail. As the ascent continues, however, the trail degenerates into a barely recognizable cairned route.

To find the route from the river, walk up the ditch at the top of 44.5 mile riffle and look for a trail climbing to your left (drainage right). This is about 75 yards off the river. The trail leads up a broken slope of Redwall for a refreshing above-the-river view. For most hikers, this is a perfect destination. If you are going for the rim, follow cairns that lead north across gently rolling terrain until arriving at a wide boulder-filled drainage where the trail splinters into a maze of rocks.

By now you should have spied your objective—an obvious notch in the rim to the north. The route simply follows the path of least resistance to that notch. It goes up the lower Supai cliff where it is eroded—on the point. This is dead ahead or slightly to your left if you are in the bouldery drainage looking at the notch. Once up the lower Supai cliff, cairns meander upslope toward the upper Supai cliffs. After traversing near the base of these upper Supai cliffs, the route begins climbing more steeply as it nears the gully coming from the notch. The last several hundred feet are a steep walk over and around huge chunks of rock that have fallen from above. Just before reaching the rim, you'll go under a block of fallen limestone that is wedged between the cliffs. A short 4th class climb (12-foot exposure) is the final challenge before standing on the rim.

To the north are views of the Echo and Vermillion Cliffs. If you are lucky enough to be here in October you can look across the canyon at the colorful aspen-studded forests of the Kaibab Plateau.

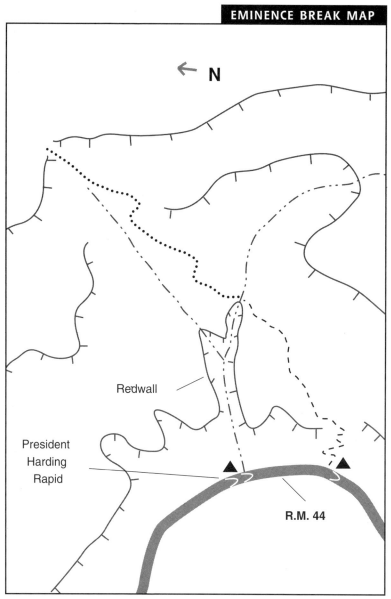

N

Redwall

President
Harding
Rapid

R.M. 44

1/4 mile

.......... route
—··—··— creekbed
- - - - trail
▲ camp
⊤⊤⊤⊤ cliff rim

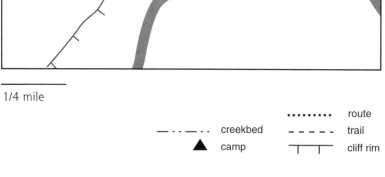

Point Hansbrough as viewed from Eminence Break

# Saddle Canyon

**River Mile:** 47.0—right
**Time:** 3 hours
**Difficulty:** Easy to Moderate. This hike follows a rugged trail.
**Wet or Dry?:** Both. This hike is mostly dry, but there are several creek crossings where a slip will have you in the water. There is also some optional wading at the end of the hike.
**Ideal Weather:** Moderate
**Potential:** A waterfall 1.4 miles from the river stops any further exploration.
**Camp:** There are two large camps at Saddle.

**Route Description:** A Saddle Canyon hike has many faces. Near the mouth, a trail leads up dry, open slopes. Next comes a wide canyon bottom graced with a creek and lush greenery. At the end of the hike, the creek rushes between narrow walls of limestone and cascades into cool waterfall-filled chambers.

From the beach at Saddle Canyon, a trail twists out the back of the campsite and up the desert slope. Initially, this is a steep climb. It can be awfully hot on a warm day. When the trail starts to level off and traverse the slope high above the creekbed, stop and take a look around. The view is awesome.

The trail will gently lead back down to the creek as you enter a valley ensconced in giant Redwall cliffs. The bottom of this broad canyon is filled with a variety of plant and animal life. Most of the trees are netleaf hackberry, but there is also boxelder and redbud. The toads you'll see launching into pools upon your approach are likely *Bufo woodhousei*, or Woodhouse toads.

Just as you're working up a good case of heat stroke from the exposed trail, relief is offered with Muav Limestone narrows. The tiny creek tumbles over bedrock ledges while deciduous trees compete fiercely for any available soil in the air-conditioned setting. The last few feet of exploration require wading in the creek. A 5th class boulder move will reveal an additional 20 yards of canyon including a moss-backed 30-foot waterfall.

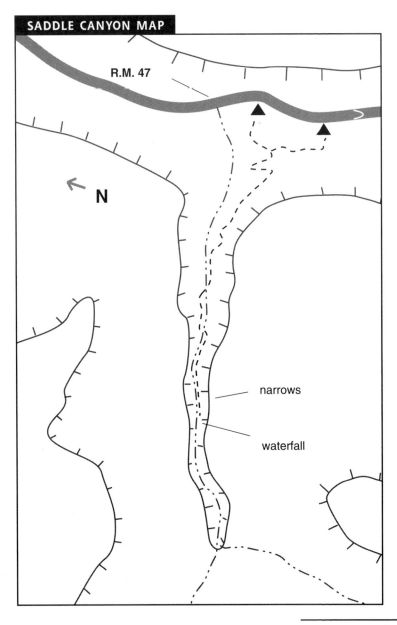

# SADDLE CANYON MAP

R.M. 47

N

narrows

waterfall

1/4 mile

......... route
- - - - - trail    —..—.. creekbed
⊤⊤ cliff rim    ▲ camp

Taking in the immensity of Marble Gorge from the Saddle Canyon trail

# Nankoweap to Kwagunt Saddle

**River Mile:** 52 to 53—right
**Time**: 6 to 8 hours round-trip to go to the saddle dividing Nankoweap and Kwagunt.
**Difficulty:** Difficult. This is a long hike any way you slice it.
**Wet or Dry?:** Dry
**Ideal Weather:** Cool
**Potential:** There are many hiking options from the Nankoweap springs.
**Camp:** There are three big camps along the Nankoweap Delta that all have access to this hike. You could also get to the saddle by starting from one of the two Kwagunt camps.

**Route Description:** A hike to the Nankoweap/Kwagunt saddle is a good destination for those who want to go a little farther than the Nankoweap springs.

The first part of this hike is the same as the standard Nankoweap Creek hike leading to springs 2.5 miles from the river. You will be hiking along Nankoweap Creek, following cairns in places but generally just making your way upstream. When the canyon opens abruptly revealing a broad valley, you have reached the Butte Fault. There are springs here—easily identified by marshy areas, mesquite trees, and a few cottonwoods.

From the springs on Nankoweap Creek, make your way south, climbing the slopes of tilted strata. There are numerous routes one can take, but the idea is to arrive at the pass between Nankoweap Butte (to the west) and the much larger Nankoweap Mesa to the east. Regardless of which route you choose, you will be hiking up steep slopes and across interesting desert scenery.

From the pass, you will have expansive views of both the Nankoweap and Kwagunt drainages. Mere mortals will return to camp via Nankoweap Creek, but mega-hike lovers might want to descend into Kwagunt Creek, walk down to the river, and then head upstream along the Colorado back to camp.

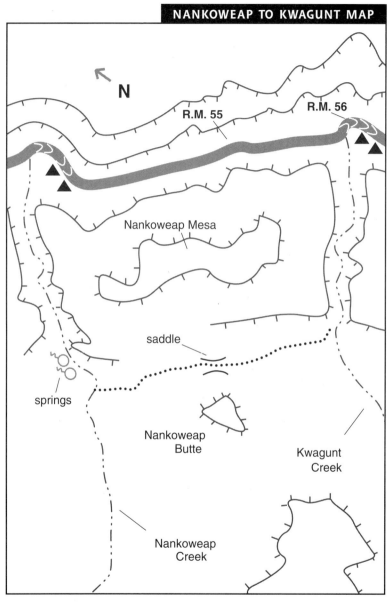

N

R.M. 55

R.M. 56

Nankoweap Mesa

saddle

springs

Nankoweap
Butte

Kwagunt
Creek

Nankoweap
Creek

1/4 mile

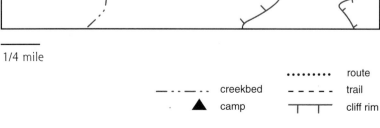

········· route

— · — · — creekbed      – – – – trail

▲ camp      ⊤⊤⊤⊤ cliff rim

53

Walking along the Nankoweap / Kwagunt saddle

# Nankoweap Creek

**River Mile:** 52 to 53—right
**Time:** 4 hours round-trip to the springs along the Butte Fault
**Difficulty:** Easy
**Wet or Dry?:** Dry. You might have to jump across Nankoweap Creek a time or two.
**Ideal Weather:** Cool or Moderate
**Potential:** You could hike forever here.
**Camp:** There are three big camps along the Nankoweap Delta that all have access to this hike. Little Nankoweap Camp at mile 51.8 also accesses the area.

**Route Description:** If you're not up for an all-day mega-hike, but you still want to stretch your legs a bit at Nankoweap, this is the hike to do. It follows relatively flat terrain for a couple of miles through a nice canyon with flowing water and finishes in an open valley with great views.

From any of the Nankoweap camps, make your way into the Nankoweap creekbed (try to stay on the most major trail leading here) and walk upstream. If you follow the cairns up the creekbed, you'll save some energy by staying on a smoother, more beaten path than the loose boulders of the riverbed. The cairned route climbs benches and bypasses a couple of boulder-choked sections of creek, but whether you're on trail or not, the basic idea is to head upstream.

The canyon never really gets narrow, but tall cliffs of Redwall and neatly-laid ledges of Muav Limestone keep it scenic. The running water is nice, too.

Judging from the wide riverbed, Nankoweap Creek sometimes floods at several thousand c.f.s., although a typical springtime flow is less than 50 c.f.s., and the rest of the year it is less than 10 c.f.s. Most of this tiny flow is supported by several springs located about 2.5 miles from the Colorado.

This area of springs serves as a turnaround point for this hike, or an embarkation point for a multitude of longer hikes in the area. The springs are identified by large marshy areas set below oaks, mesquite, and cottonwoods. The springs are located on the Butte Fault, an easily recognizable feature. The canyon you have been enjoying stops abruptly here, and the terrain opens into a broad valley. If you gain some elevation above the creek, you will be rewarded with liberating views of the Nankoweap Basin. Mount Hayden proudly sits as an impressive sandstone spire on the horizon, and dense fir forests pour off the Kaibab Plateau to the west. From here, you can begin a number of routes that lead farther into the canyon, or head back to the river.

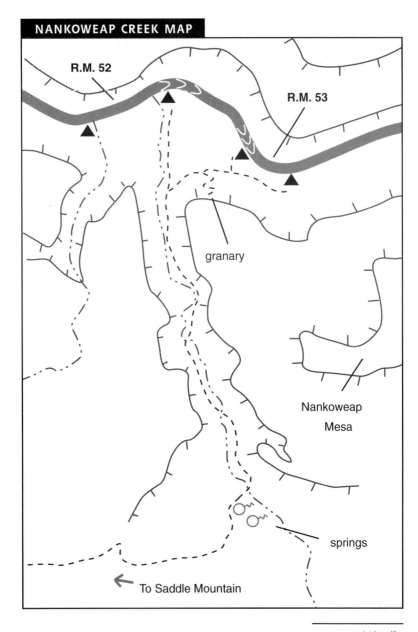

# NANKOWEAP CREEK MAP

R.M. 52

R.M. 53

granary

Nankoweap
Mesa

springs

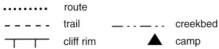

← To Saddle Mountain

1/4 mile

| | | |
|---|---|---|
| ......... route | | |
| - - - - - trail | - .. - .. - | creekbed |
| ⊤⊤⊤ cliff rim | ▲ | camp |

What! You call this a canyon?

# Nankoweap Granaries

**River Mile:** 52.6—right
**Time:** 1 hour, 30 minutes
**Difficulty:** Easy to Moderate. This is a short hike on a trail, but it is steep. Bad knees will not like the descent.
**Wet or Dry?:** Dry
**Ideal Weather:** Cool or Moderate
**Potential:** This trail stops at the cliffside granaries, but there are numerous hiking options up Nankoweap Creek.
**Camp:** Any of the Nankoweap camps between miles 52 and 53 are fine. This is a popular area for backpackers as well as river runners.

**Route Description:** A hike to the granaries above the Nankoweap Delta is a Grand Canyon classic. The main attraction here is a prehistoric ruin, but even if you aren't interested in the archeology the hike is still worthwhile because of the great downstream view.

From any of the Nankoweap camps, find your way to the trail that connects the different camps, located at the base of the slope. Try to stay on the main routes to avoid multiple trailing. Follow this connector trail until a spur trail heads up to the granaries. This spur-trail junction is located about halfway up the hill that is to the south of Nankoweap Creek. It is easiest to find your way if you locate the granaries from the river first. They appear as four small holes in the Redwall to the south of Nankoweap Creek.

The trail leading up to the granaries is well used but steep. Stick it out—the top will reward you with a famous and photogenic downstream view.

The granaries were used to store seeds for beans and squash. The Puebloans farmed the Nankoweap Delta in addition to gathering mesquite "beans" and other meager nutritional sources of the desert.

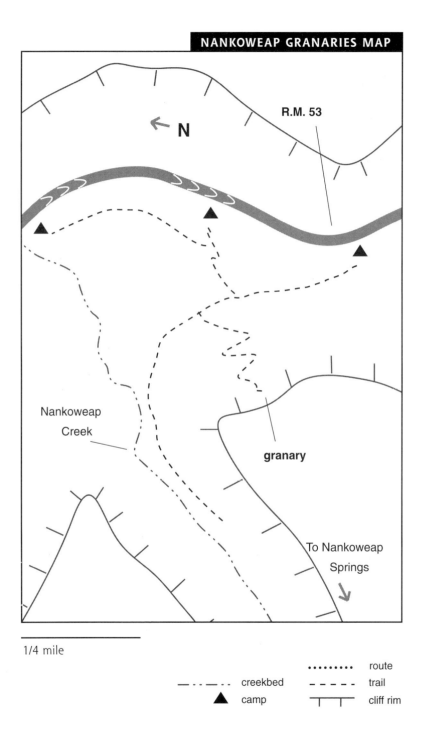

R.M. 53

← N

Nankoweap
Creek

granary

To Nankoweap
Springs

1/4 mile

route

creekbed

camp

trail

cliff rim

A granary with a view

# Kwagunt Creek

**River Mile:** 56.0—right
**Time:** 2.5 to 3 hours to the Butte Fault area
**Difficulty:** Moderate
**Wet or Dry?:** Dry. Though there is often water in the creek, it is easily avoidable.
**Ideal Weather:** Cool or Moderate
**Potential:** From the Butte Fault area, energetic hikers can explore far and wide. Nankoweap Butte and the upper Kwagunt Valley are both good destinations.
**Camp:** There are two big camps at the mouth of Kwagunt.

**Route Description:** Kwagunt is the sister creek to Nankoweap. Both drainages emanate from the fir forests of the eastern Kaibab Plateau, flow through broad valleys, then cross the Butte Fault before squeezing through canyons to the river. If you're looking for an alternative to the popular Nankoweap area, this is it.

Kwagunt Creek has created a large alluvial fan at its mouth that is now mostly covered in mesquite. At the northern edge of this fan runs the creek, providing the easiest walking for upstream exploration. The walking is mostly easy and flat, but there are a few places where hikers are forced to find routes around giant boulders blocking the creekbed. (Climbers take note: the giant boulders scattered in this creekbed offer some nice bouldering.) On warm days, small bluffs of Muav Limestone can provide welcome shade in the otherwise brutally exposed creekbed.

About an hour and a half of upstream hiking will bring you to the Kwagunt Valley. You'll know when you're there, it really is a valley. If you get some elevation above the creekbed the views are impressive. Towering spires and buttes rim the valley, creating an exotic landscape. The terrain is open, and the hiking options are limitless. Bring your topographic map and have fun!

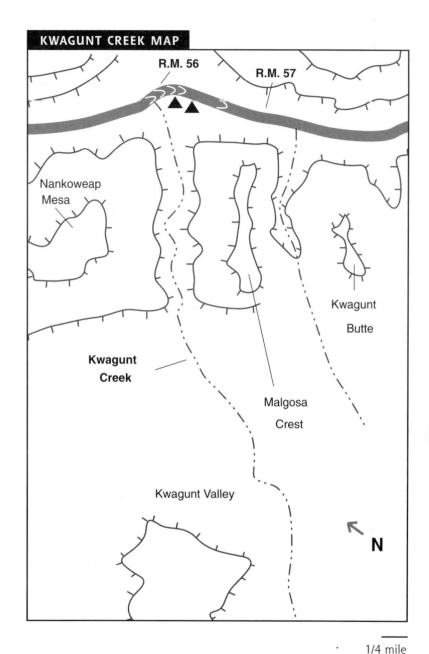

# KWAGUNT CREEK MAP

R.M. 56

R.M. 57

Nankoweap
Mesa

Kwagunt
Butte

Kwagunt
Creek

Malgosa
Crest

Kwagunt Valley

N

1/4 mile

........ route
— — — — trail    —··—·· creekbed
⊤⊤⊤ cliff rim    ▲ camp

Looking up Kwagunt Valley

# Little Colorado River

**River Mile:** 61.3—left
**Time:** A one-mile hike up the Little Colorado takes 1 to 2 hours round-trip.
**Difficulty:** Easy
**Wet or Dry:** Wet. The warm azure water of the L.C.R. is what makes it special. Embrace it.
**Ideal Weather:** Any. Obviously, it is nicer to swim here when it is hot.
**Potential:** The Little Colorado River Canyon snakes along for nearly 50 miles.
**Camp:** Camping at the L.C.R. is illegal, but there are several camps within five miles upstream on the big Colorado.

**Route Description:** The Little Colorado River drains a substantial portion of the Southwest. A drainage of this size would normally flow several thousand cubic feet per second were it in the Eastern U.S., but here in the parched desert Southwest we are left with a modest 200 c.f.s. But what a wonderful 200 c.f.s. it is. The Little Colorado is rich in dissolved calcium carbonate which produces a beautiful turquoise water color more reminiscent of the Caribbean than the desert. The chemically vibrant water forms travertine ledges that the Little Colorado tumbles over in a playful dance on its way to the big river.

Hiking here is best done when the water is its usual stunning blue, not when it is a flood-induced chocolate brown. The Little Colorado swells into a big river at times—usually in March, April, or May—from snowmelt. Brief periods of high water also occur from summer thunderstorms. In September 1923, the U.S.G.S. party was camped at Lava Falls when they saw the river quickly rise to an estimated 112,000 c.f.s. It is believed that most of that flow was coming from the Little Colorado!

Sidewalks of Tapeats Sandstone lead up the river right side of the L.C.R. for the first few hundred yards, and then a trail develops. About 0.4 miles up from the boats, a class I rapid makes an exciting swimming hole. It's a fun game to swim in these temperate waters after dealing with the ferocious and cold water of the big river. Be careful of the sharp travertine riverbed in the Little Colorado. It is a good idea to wear a life jacket around your waist like a diaper when swimming through the rapids here.

Trails continue up both sides of the river for a couple of miles, and then they fade, making for difficult walking through tamarisks. The scenery stays much the same—towering cliffs and a running stream.

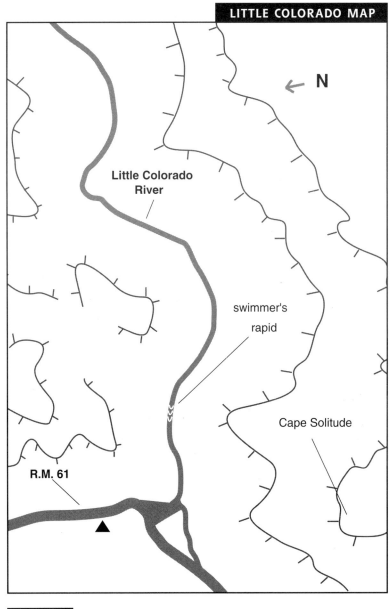

← N

Little Colorado
River

swimmer's
rapid

Cape Solitude

R.M. 61

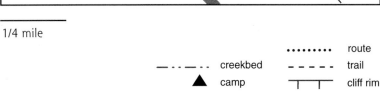

1/4 mile

— ·· — ·· — creekbed     ·········· route

▲ camp     − − − − trail

cliff rim

Lisa Gelezis

Confuence of the Little C and Big C

# Walter Powell Route

**River Mile:** 61.3—left
**Time:** 6 to 10 hours for a strong party to go to the rim and back.
**Difficulty:** Difficult. This is a long and complex route with lots of walking over rugged sidehill terrain. Because camping is not allowed at the Little Colorado, this route is barely feasible as a day hike from the river. Experienced and fit canyon hikers who are ready for an adventure are the only ones who should even consider this route.
**Wet or Dry?:** Dry
**Ideal Weather:** Cool
**Potential:** From the top of the route, a 10-minute walk to the west will provide an awesome view.
**Camp:** There are a few small to medium camps between Kwagunt and the L.C.R. Camping is not allowed at the Little Colorado.

**Route Description:** According to Powell's journal, Walter Powell (John Wesley's brother) used this route to go to the rim for a barometer reading in 1869. "Captain Powell early in the morning takes a barometer and goes out to climb a point between the two rivers." Walter must have been a gnarly dude, because this is a demanding route. Today, all the crux spots on the route are cairned unless L.B. has been there recently to kick them over.

From the mouth of the Little Colorado, walk upstream about 0.5 miles to where there is a 30-foot high arch on river right. The arch is hard to see, so look closely. The route starts its arduous course to the rim here, on the downstream side of the arch. Head straight uphill toward the base of the most prominent Redwall cliff in the vicinity. The first cliffs you will encounter have a couple routes through them, the easiest being a minor 4th class scramble. Once through this first band, traverse left staying close to the base of the Redwall face until you are nearly in a gully.

The next portion of the route is pretty obvious. Go up the steep hillside adjacent to the gully, climbing a 4th class bluff of Redwall en-route. A couple hundred feet above the climb, start angling left for a saddle that overlooks a Little Colorado side drainage to the east. From this saddle, you can see the remainder of the route. It traverses the steep boulder-strewn slopes in the foreground until reaching the big gully with house-sized boulders at the head of the drainage. The route then goes straight up this gully to the lowest spot on the rim.

When you near the top of the talus at the head of the drainage, veer slightly left into the gateway canyon of Coconino Sandstone. This upper canyon contains the final challenges. A few short 5th class moves will finally have you on the freedom of the rim—3,280 feet above the river.

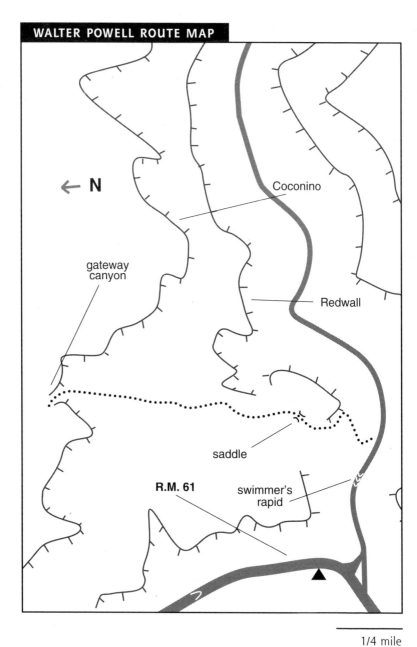

WALTER POWELL ROUTE MAP

← N

Coconino

gateway
canyon

Redwall

saddle

R.M. 61    swimmer's
rapid

1/4 mile

········· route
– – – – – trail          –··–··– creekbed
⊤ ⊤ ⊤ cliff rim        ▲ camp

68

This awesome view is found at the top of the Walter Powell route.

# Carbon–Lava Loop

**River Mile:** 64.5 to 65.5—right
**Time:** 2 hours
**Difficulty:** Easy to Moderate. Although there is a trail most of the way, there are also a couple of scrambles.
**Wet or Dry?:** Dry. There is a small flow in Lava Creek.
**Ideal Weather:** Cool. This hike is terribly exposed—scorching on a hot day.
**Potential:** There are all-day hikes up both Carbon and Lava creeks.
**Camp:** There are small camps at Carbon Creek and Lava Creek, and several more camps just downstream—Palisades at 65.8, Espejo at 66.8, Tanner at 68.5, and Basalt at 69.4.

**Route Description:** This is a great hike that goes up a narrow canyon, across an open valley, and down a small creek. The most difficult part of doing this is figuring out the logistics. A short boat shuttle is required for this route, so some members of your party will have to float the boats downstream while the rest hike.

From the mouth of Carbon Creek, the first part of the route leads up a dry boulder-filled creekbed. There is one short 4th class scramble around a fall, but the rest is boulder hopping and simple walking. About 0.7 miles from the river, there is a huge rockslide on your left (creek right). Look for the cairned trail leading up the slide and take it to the top, where the canyon takes an unexpected 90 degree turn into Tapeats narrows.

The narrows drift along for about 0.5 miles until they abruptly end at the Butte Fault. The normally horizontal Tapeats Sandstone bends radically upward into a vertical plane. After studying this amazing geology, take the trail to the left, entering the rounded and colorful desert of the Chuar Valley. Hiking the open terrain is a liberating experience after traveling the claustrophobic depths of Marble Gorge.

The trail leads slightly uphill, and then down a sandy wash amidst a psychedelic moonscape. Greens, purples, ochres, and reds twist and roll in a ribbon of soils. This beautiful descent continues until just above Lava Creek, when the route takes one last detour to the left. The trail goes over a small hill here, avoiding a fall in the wash. Continuing downstream, you'll soon be along the clear trickle of Lava Creek. This desert creek will accompany you to the river, where your boat should be waiting at the top of Lava-Chuar Rapid.

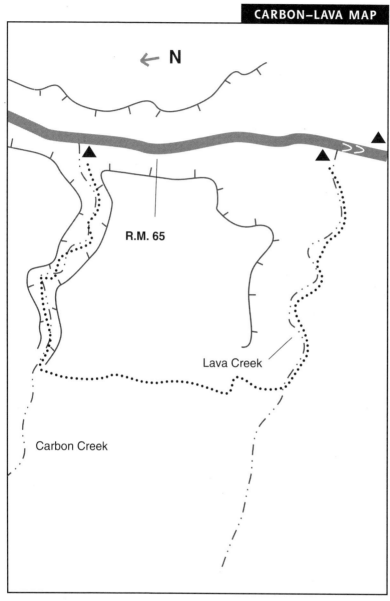

← N

R.M. 65

Lava Creek

Carbon Creek

1/4 mile

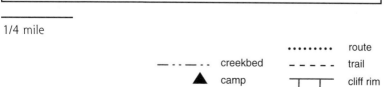

| | | |
|---|---|---|
| ·········· route | | |
| –·–·–·· creekbed | – – – – trail | |
| ▲ camp | ┬─┬─┬ cliff rim | |

Chuar Valley

# Tanner Trail

**River Mile:** 68.5—left
**Time:** 4 to 7 hours to the rim. An hour hike up the trail will gain nice views.
**Difficulty:** Easy to Moderate. This is a steep trail.
**Wet or Dry?:** Dry. There is no water on this route.
**Ideal Weather:** Cool
**Potential:** The Tanner Trail leads to the rim. Adventurous hikers might want to attempt a scramble up Cardenas Butte.
**Camp:** A couple of hundred yards upstream from Tanner Rapid, there are camps on both sides of the river. Obviously, the river left camp is better for hiking the Tanner Trail, but you may have to share the area with backpackers. It is relatively easy to ferry across the river from the river right camps to the Tanner Trail.

**Route Description:** The Tanner Trail leads from the top of Tanner Rapid to Lipan Point on the South Rim, offering spacious views of the colorful and vast Furnace Flats region en-route. This 7.6 (it seems much longer) mile trail can serve as a good route out of the Canyon for those who must leave the river before Phantom Ranch.

There is a willow and tamarisk-covered beach area on river left at the head of Tanner Rapid that is used for camping, mainly by backpackers. The Tanner Trail starts here, and leads up onto a low bench, where it forks at a junction with the Beamer Trail. The Beamer Trail goes north along the river to the Little Colorado. The Tanner forks right, crosses the wash (follow the cairns here), and begins a long ascending traverse up the western slopes of Tanner Canyon.

The turnaround point on this hike is arbitrary. The higher you go, the better the view. If you are going for the rim, prepare yourself for a steep climb through the Redwall. After this, the trail flattens as it contours across two big bowls below Cardenas and Escalante Buttes. From the Seventy-five mile saddle near Escalante Butte, it is two more steep miles to the rim.

This route has been in use since ancient times as a way to cross the Canyon. The trail was named after Seth Tanner, a miner who re-constructed the indian route in the late 1800s in order to reach copper mines near the river.

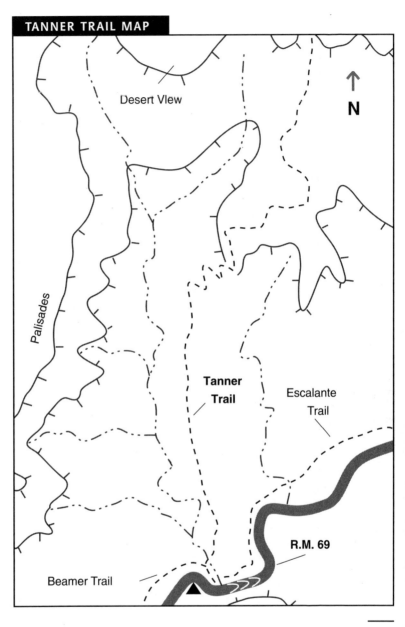

# TANNER TRAIL MAP

Desert View

N

Palisades

**Tanner Trail**

Escalante Trail

R.M. 69

Beamer Trail

1/4 mile

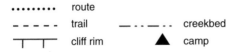

......... route

- - - - - trail         —··— creekbed

┬┬┬ cliff rim    ▲ camp

A keen eye views the landscape from the Tanner Trail.

# Hilltop Ruin

**River Mile:** 71.0—left
**Time:** 1 hour, 20 minutes to the ruin and back.
**Difficulty:** Easy. This is a short uphill trail hike.
**Wet or Dry?:** Dry
**Ideal Weather:** Cool or Moderate
**Potential:** From Hilltop Ruin, one could follow the Escalante Trail/Route upstream or downstream for several miles.
**Camp:** Cardenas Camp is the start of this hike. There are also camps on both sides of the river at Basalt (mile 69).

**Route Description:** This is a trail hike to a Puebloan ruin. Over the years, the ruin has been reconstructed to such an extent that it no longer has an authentic feel, but with some imagination, it is still a neat place to contemplate Grand Canyon's human history. There are also great views of Furnace Flats and the Palisades from this hike.

The hike begins at Cardenas Camp. The ruin is on the rounded hilltop southwest of camp. A trail leads out of Cardenas Camp and intersects the Escalante Trail about 180 yards from the river. Take a right here, and follow the Escalante Trail gradually uphill and downstream. In another 60 yards the spur trail you're looking for cuts left, switch-backing upslope toward Hilltop Ruin.

This is a hot and dry hike all the way. It's a good way to warm up in the winter and a scorcher in the summer. Springtime winds often blow incessantly in this open part of Grand Canyon. Though they are an enemy on the river, they can bring welcome relief from the heat on the Hilltop Ruin hike. As one surveys the view from the hilltop, it is obvious why this portion of the river is known as Furnace Flats. The vertical sandstone and limestone canyons of Marble Gorge have been replaced here with shadeless washes scattered across a colorful and desolate landscape.

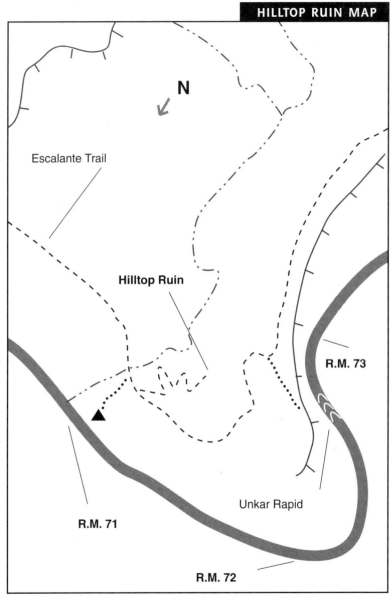

N

Escalante Trail

Hilltop Ruin

R.M. 73

R.M. 71

Unkar Rapid

R.M. 72

1/4 mile

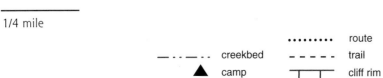

········ route

—··—··— creekbed    ----- trail

▲ camp    ⊤⊤⊤ cliff rim

Hiking near Hilltop Ruin
(Notice Solomon Temple and the Tabernacle in the background.)

# The Tabernacle

**River Mile:** 74.1—right
**Time:** 5 to 6 hours
**Difficulty:** Moderate. It is 2,200 vertical feet from the river to the top of the Tabernacle.
**Wet or Dry?:** Dry
**Ideal Weather:** Cool
**Potential:** This route leads to the top of a prominent butte from which miles of potential routes are visible.
**Camp:** Rattlesnake Camp just below the mile 74 drainage on river right is best. There is also a ledge camp 100 yards upstream from Rattlesnake.

**Route Description:** The Tabernacle is the perfect hike for someone who wants to get a lofty view of the eastern Grand Canyon without doing any rock climbing. A trail leads all the way to the top of this ideal butte.

The route starts from the back of Rattlesnake Camp. This is on the downstream side of the drainage at mile 74, just before the river makes a left turn. If you aren't camped at Rattlesnake, you can reach this route from upstream or downstream by hiking along shore. Look for some big table-sized slabs of rock leaning against the small cliff at the upstream end of camp. There are cairns leading you away from the beach, but they are hardly necessary. This route has gotten popular enough in recent years to develop its own trail. Stay on it.

The trail climbs steeply from the river, but soon mellows into a gradual ascent along a narrow ridge. The ridge broadens into a rounded desert slope as the trail continues along it, leading towards a point of broken Tapeats Sandstone. The trail meanders through the Tapeats, then streaks across a relatively flat section before traversing around to the east and then the north side of the Tabernacle. The final approach to the summit leads up the north and northwestern sides of the butte. At the top you are rewarded with a spectacular view of the South Rim, Furnace Flats, Solomon Temple, the Palisades and Unkar Rapid. You can even hear the roar of the rapid far below unless the tourist helicopters are near.

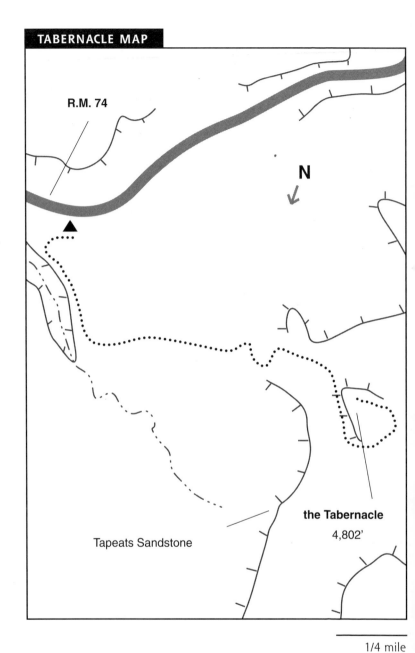

## TABERNACLE MAP

R.M. 74

N

the Tabernacle
4,802'

Tapeats Sandstone

1/4 mile

········· route

– – – – – trail  –··–··– creekbed

⊤⊤⊤ cliff rim  ▲ camp

View of Solomon Temple from the Tabernacle

# Vishnu Creek

**River Mile:** 81.1—right
**Time:** 30 minutes to a difficult climb and back. Longer if you make the climb.
**Difficulty:** Difficult. Most of the route involves climbing.
**Wet or Dry?:** Wet
**Ideal Weather:** Moderate or Hot
**Potential:** There appear to be possible routes through the Tapeats here.
**Camp:** Grapevine is a medium-sized camp directly across the river from Vishnu Creek. However, this camp should be left for trips that are doing exchanges at Phantom.

**Route Description:** Not many river runners will get the opportunity to do this hike, because the eddy you must catch to walk up Vishnu Creek is small and hard to catch. The best chance rafts have at stopping here would be to pull in on river right about 100 yards upstream from Grapevine camp and try to scramble downstream over steep granite to the creekbed of Vishnu. Kayakers camped at Grapevine can ferry directly across the river in order to hike at Vishnu Creek. Don't miss the eddy.

Once you have survived getting to the mouth of Vishnu, you'll find it to be a pretty cool place. Twisting metamorphic narrows lead away from the river in reality-bending curves. A small stream of clear water slides down chutes and into gorgeous pools. The walking is up the creekbed. If you don't want to get wet in the pools, you'll have to do some climbing.

The first climb is a 4th class scramble around a pool only 75 yards from the river. If you make it past this first obstacle, you'll do fine for the next 0.4 miles, where you'll reach a small waterfall with a pool below it. The only way to proceed is to climb a short but steep face of schist on creek left. The exposure is virtually nil, but the difficulty of the move is about a 5.8 nonetheless, so only decent rock climbers will be able to make it past this point. If you don't make it, no worries—you've already seen the best scenery of the canyon.

Above the difficult falls, the metamorphic narrows continue for about 0.3 miles, and then the canyon opens up a little. There are several gullies near here that could serve as quick routes up to the Tapeats and a good view of the inner gorge.

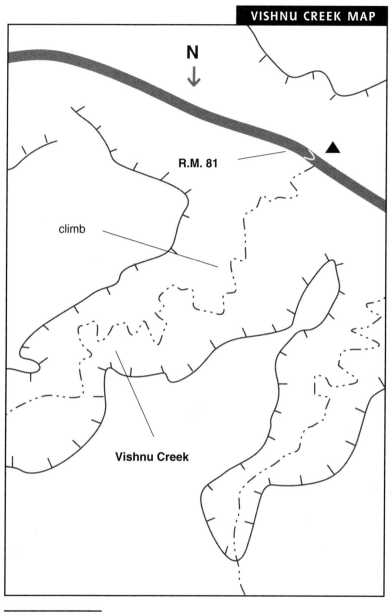

## VISHNU CREEK MAP

N
↓

R.M. 81

climb

Vishnu Creek

1/4 mile

creekbed ⋯⋯⋯ route

▲ camp — — — trail

┬┬┬ cliff rim

# Clear Creek

**River Mile:** 84.1—river right
**Time:** 1 hour to the waterfall and back
**Difficulty:** Easy to Moderate. Getting across the schist at the river requires some 3rd class scrambling. Once in the creekbed, it's easy.
**Wet or Dry?:** Wet
**Ideal Weather:** Moderate or Hot
**Potential:** About 4.5 miles up Clear Creek you will hit the Clear Creek Trail that comes over from Phantom Ranch.
**Camp:** Grapevine Camp is 3 miles upstream, and there are two camps at Cremation 1.5 miles downstream. However, these camps should be left for trips doing exchanges at Phantom Ranch.

**Route Description:** Clear Creek is a classic Grand Canyon river hike. Narrows and a clear stream running through schist make this a popular stop in the inner gorge.

Boat parking for Clear Creek is tricky. Kayaks can catch the powerful eddy right at the mouth of Clear Creek, but rafts and dories should pull over 100 yards upstream where the river is calm. At mile 84, just when you can see a small rapid downstream, pull in along the polished schist on river right. From here you must scramble downstream over the narrow fins of bedrock until you reach Clear Creek.

Walking upstream in the creekbed, you'll either be in the ankle-deep creek or on the rounded cobbles adjacent to the creek. Smooth black walls soon frame the creek in a beautiful little canyon, and every turn reveals a new scene more intriguing than the last.

About 0.5 miles up from the river, there is a lovely waterfall that serves as a good turnaround point. You can scramble around the falls on creek right if you want to keep going. Clear Creek eventually leads to a nice backpacking trail 4.5 miles up from the river. From here, the trail leads across the Tonto platform 9 miles to Phantom Ranch.

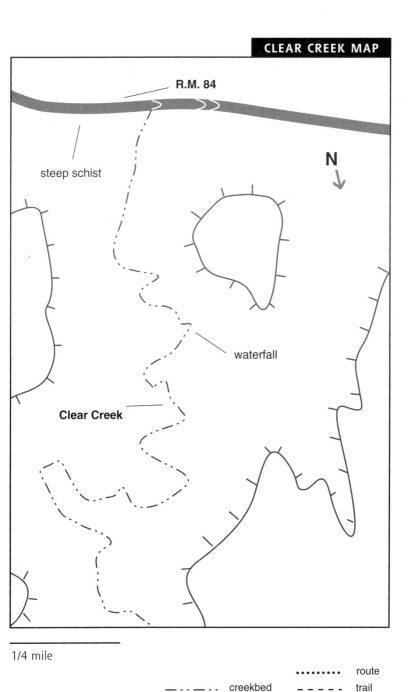

R.M. 84

steep schist

N

waterfall

**Clear Creek**

1/4 mile

creekbed
camp

route
trail
cliff rim

The waterfall on Clear Creek

# South Kaibab Trail

**River Mile:** 87.5—right
**Time:** 3 to 7 hours to the rim one way
**Difficulty:** Easy. It is all uphill, but the trail is big and smooth.
**Wet or Dry:?** Dry
**Ideal Weather:** Cool
**Potential:** Aerobic junkies could do a great loop run here: Up the Kaibab to the top of the inner gorge, across the Tonto to Indian Gardens, and then down the Bright Angel and back to the river.
**Camp:** The best camps for making exchanges at Phantom are Cremation and Grapevine.

**Route Description:** The South Kaibab Trail is shorter, steeper, and a bit less crowded than the Bright Angel. It is 6.3 miles from the Kaibab Suspension Bridge to the South Rim. Compare this to the 9.2 miles of the Bright Angel, and you can see why this is the preferred route of river guides hiking in or out of the Canyon from Phantom. Be forewarned: almost every step of the way is up. The South Kaibab gains 380 vertical feet more than the Bright Angel, finishing at 7,200 feet above sea level.

The South Kaibab is steep, but it makes up for that by being exposed and dry, too. Whereas the Bright Angel has fresh water halfway up and shade periodically along its length, the Kaibab is exposed to full sun and the nearest water is the Colorado River.

Still think the South Kaibab is the route for you? Great, you'll love it. The views from the lip of the inner gorge are awesome, and they only get better farther up. After a gradual climb to the base of the Redwall, the trail switchbacks up to the crest of Cedar Ridge, with spacious panoramas both east and west across the heart of Grand Canyon. Near the top you'll pass a couple of random Douglas fir trees growing in the shade of the rim—a welcome contrast to the scorching desert below.

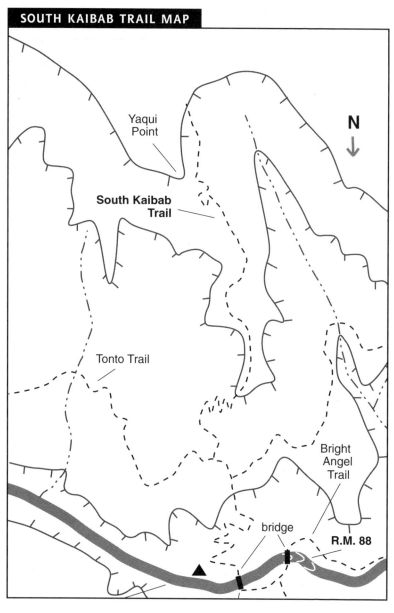

# SOUTH KAIBAB TRAIL MAP

Yaqui
Point

**South Kaibab
Trail**

N

Tonto Trail

Bright
Angel
Trail

bridge

**R.M. 88**

1/4 mile

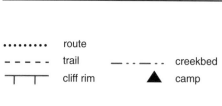

•••••••• route

– – – – – trail   –··–··– creekbed

⊤⊤⊤⊤ cliff rim   ▲ camp

South Kaibab Trail

# Bright Angel Trail

**River Mile:** 87.8—right
**Time:** 4 to 8 hours one way to the South Rim
**Difficulty:** Easy. Though a hike to the rim climbs nearly 5,000 vertical feet, the trail is wide and relatively smooth all the way.
**Wet or Dry?:** Dry
**Ideal Weather:** Cool
**Potential:** For someone who is more into hiking than floating, an Indian Gardens to Monument Creek hike along the Tonto Trail is a spectacular way to avoid Horn Creek Rapid.
**Camp:** Grapevine or Cremation are the nearest camps for doing exchanges at Phantom Ranch.

**Route Description:** Phantom Ranch is the most common place along the river to do exchanges with river trip participants. Some people end their trip here with a 9-mile hike to the South Rim, while others begin their river trip by hiking in and immediately running some of Grand Canyon's biggest whitewater.

There are two choices for people hiking between Phantom Ranch and the South Rim: the Bright Angel and the South Kaibab Trails. For a steep and direct route out of the Canyon, the Kaibab is the best choice, but for easier hiking and more convenience, the Bright Angel wins.

The Bright Angel is the most heavily used trail in Grand Canyon. In fact, so many different people hike here that one can judge his progress by the type of footwear encountered on the way up. Near the river, you'll likely see only sturdy hiking boots. Halfway up the hill at Indian Gardens, you may begin to see sneakers on some of your fellow hikers. You know that you're close to the rim when you see adventurous cityphiles in fine white pumps.

Don't let the heavy traffic fool you, though, the Bright Angel is still a healthy walk. After crossing the silver bridge downstream from the mouth of Bright Angel Creek, the trail follows the river downstream for a mile to Pipe Creek before starting its climb to the rim. Three miles and 1,300 feet above the river is the welcome oasis of Indian Gardens—a shady cottonwood grove complete with fresh drinking water, trailside benches, and a ranger station. Yes, you are nearing civilization. From Indian Gardens it is five more steep miles to the bustle of Grand Canyon Village and a good dose of culture shock.

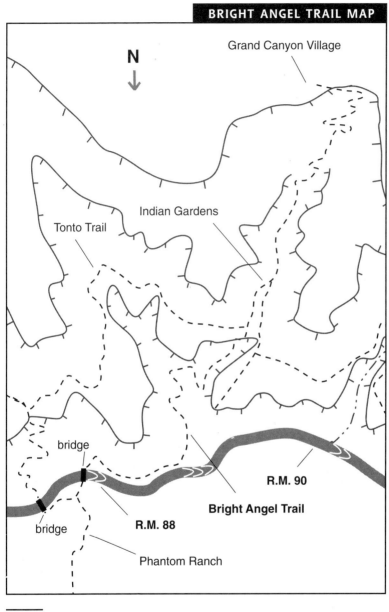

N

Grand Canyon Village

Indian Gardens

Tonto Trail

bridge

R.M. 90

Bright Angel Trail

bridge

R.M. 88

Phantom Ranch

1/4 mile

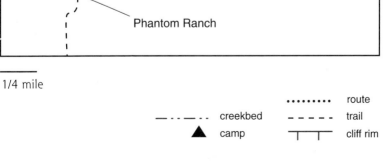

— · · — · · —  creekbed

▲  camp

· · · · · · · ·  route

— — — —  trail

┬───┬  cliff rim

91

# Monument Creek

**River Mile:** 93.5—left
**Time:** 1 hour 30 minutes to the monument and back
**Difficulty:** Easy
**Wet or Dry?:** Dry to the monument. If you explore the narrows, you'll likely get your feet wet.
**Ideal Weather:** Any
**Potential:** This route leads to the Tonto Trail—a flat trail leading many miles both east and west.
**Camp:** Granite Rapid and camp is located at the mouth of Monument Creek. There is enough room for two camps here. Backpackers like to camp in this area.

**Route Description:** If you're camped at Granite, make a point to wake up early and take a morning walk up Monument Creek. You'll be glad you did. A relatively short hike will take you to a scenic sandstone tower that sits above some quaint granite narrows.

From Granite Rapid, you'll be walking up a dry cobble and gravel riverbed. If you are able to lift your eyes from the ankle-twisting rocks underfoot, you can see every major layer of Grand Canyon geology, from the schist at river level to the Kaibab Limestone on the rim.

About 0.8 miles up from the river, look for a drainage coming in on your right (creek left) with some cairns. From here, you can see the spire of Tapeats Sandstone that gives Monument Creek its name. To get a closer view of the monument, follow the cairns up the side drainage for about 75 yards, where a trail climbs the slope to your left (creek right). This trail switchbacks uphill a couple hundred yards to the monument.

From here, you can either return the way you came, or continue another 50 yards to the Tonto Trail, follow it to the head of the narrows, and go downstream through a scenic granite narrows with running water. It's a fun game to try and keep your feet dry by dancing from wall to wall in the narrows.

Below the narrows, you'll be back in the dry creekbed that will lead you back to camp.

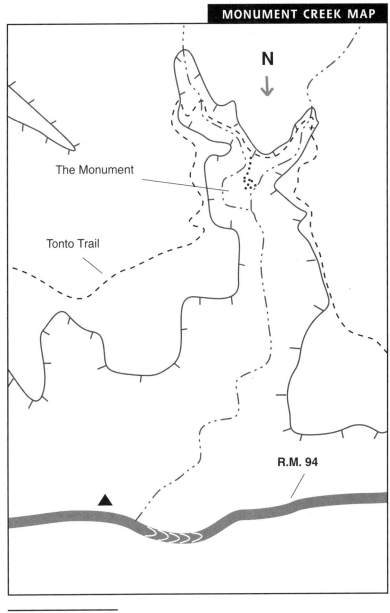

N

The Monument

Tonto Trail

R.M. 94

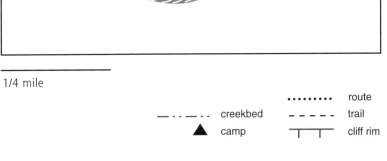

1/4 mile

| | |
|---|---|
| —··—··— creekbed | •••••••• route |
| ▲ camp | — — — trail |
| | ┬┬┬ cliff rim |

The monument of Monument Creek

# Hermit Creek

**River Mile:** 94.9—left
**Time:** 2 hours
**Difficulty:** Moderate
**Wet or Dry?:** Wet. There is a perennial stream here, but if you are determined to keep your feet dry, you can.
**Ideal Weather:** Moderate
**Potential:** This hike leads to the Tonto Trail—a flat trail that leads both east and west for many miles.
**Camp:** Hermit Camp is mid-sized, on the left above the rapid. You might have to share the area with backpackers.

**Route Description:** The rapid here is more spectacular than the hike, but if you have the time, a hike up Hermit Creek will reward you with a clear-running stream and some good across-the-river views.

There is a backpacker's camp about 1.3 miles up Hermit Creek. Most hikers camp in this campground and then day hike to the river and back. The result of this use is a trail that crosses the trickling stream of Hermit Creek several times. You can either stick with this trail or just stay in the creekbed on your way upstream. The trail becomes obvious as Tapeats Sandstone wraps the creek in a shady canyon about a mile from the river. The huge chunks of sandstone that have fallen into the creek here are the size of your basic apartment building—quite impressive.

Not far beyond the giant rocks, the trail climbs a bench and enters the backpacker's campground. This serves as the turnaround point.

If you are truly in quest of a view, ten more minutes of uphill hiking will have you into the open and scenic expanses of the Tonto platform above the inner gorge.

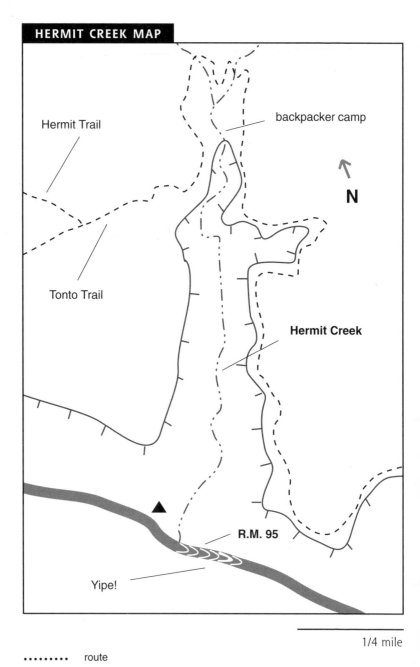

# HERMIT CREEK MAP

Hermit Trail

backpacker camp

N

Tonto Trail

Hermit Creek

R.M. 95

Yipe!

•••••••• route
– – – trail
⊤⊤⊤ cliff rim

–··–··– creekbed
▲ camp

1/4 mile

A hungry Hermit

# South Bass Trail

**River Mile:** 107.8—left
**Time:** 3 hours to get good views of the North Rim and return to the river.
**Difficulty:** Easy to Moderate. The vague trail here might require some route finding.
**Wet or Dry?:** Dry
**Ideal Weather:** Cool
**Potential:** The South Bass Trail leads to the rim.
**Camp:** Ross Wheeler Camp is nice, big, and right at the trailhead.

**Route Description:** William Wallace Bass was an industrious pioneer of the Grand Canyon tourist trade. In the 1880s, he built a home on the south rim and began leading adventurous tourists into the Canyon. Bass introduced people to Grand Canyon for nearly 40 years before he had to sell his business to the larger Fred Harvey Company in 1923. Among Bass' clientele were Thomas Moran, John Muir, and Zane Grey. The trail Bass used to reach the bottom of the Canyon was the one he had built himself—the South Bass Trail.

To find the South Bass Trail from the river, look for an old metal boat laying in the rocks. This boat is the Ross Wheeler—abandoned in 1915 when an ill-fated river trip led by the flamboyant Charles Russell finally called it quits and hiked out the South Bass Trail.

From the Ross Wheeler, the trail begins as a steep cairned route leading up the rocky slope toward the desert above. At the top of the river gorge, you'll intersect a trail that parallels the river. To go up the South Bass Trail, turn left and walk upstream. In less than a mile, you will reach the creekbed of Bass Canyon. The trail basically follows this creekbed for the next couple of miles. Cairns will direct you around several falls in the creekbed as you ascend. The turnaround point is arbitrary. The farther you go, the better the view. It is 8 miles from the river to the rim.

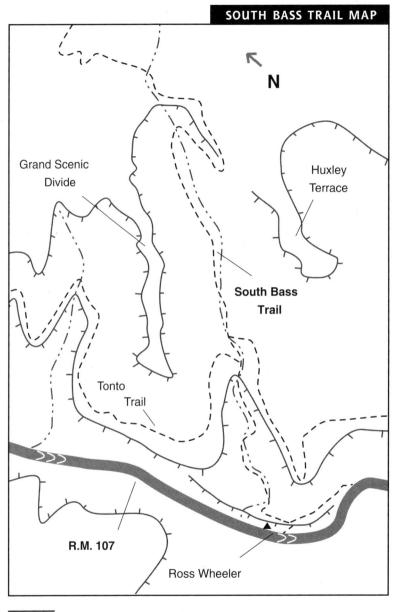

N

Grand Scenic
Divide

Huxley
Terrace

**South Bass
Trail**

Tonto
Trail

R.M. 107

Ross Wheeler

1/4 mile

·········  route

—··—··—  creekbed      — — —  trail

▲  camp      ⊤⊤⊤  cliff rim

A river party explores the South Bass.

# North Bass Trail

**River Mile:** 108.2—right
**Time:** 5 hours to the mining camp and back
**Difficulty:** Easy to the mining camp under normal conditions. If Shinumo Creek is high, this hike is moderate to difficult.
**Wet or Dry?:** Dry. However, if Shinumo Creek is high, you'll likely get wet crossing it.
**Ideal Weather:** Cool or Moderate
**Potential:** The North Bass Trail leads 12 miles to the rim.
**Camp:** Bass or Upper Bass Camps are best.

**Route Description:** The North Bass Trail traverses the spectacular and convoluted drainage af Shinumo Creek. The trail starts at the river, climbs north over a pass, and descends to Shinumo Creek. From here it follows the creek to White Canyon, where it starts a climb to a place on the North Rim called Swamp Point.

From Bass camp, the trail heads slightly upstream and uphill across the always warm south-facing desert slope. Strong hikers will reach a pass 650 feet above the river in about 30 minutes. The views from here are great. To the north, Shinumo creek is visible, with the pine-clad Powell Plateau looming in the not-too-far distance.

From the pass, the trail goes downhill to Shinumo Creek, then starts upstream along the rushing cottonwood-lined watercourse. The trail crosses the creek several times, a task that is difficult or even impossible when the water is high.

About 2.5 miles from the river, the trail passes an area called Bass Camp (not to be confused with the Bass camp at the river), a good turnaround spot and a point of interest for history buffs. In the early 1900s, William Bass guided hunters and other adventurous types into Grand Canyon. He also mined asbestos and copper. The relics from this era are left behind here at Bass Camp.

If you decide to press on upstream beyond Bass Camp, the next good landmark is White Canyon. This scenic side canyon comes in on creek right with a clear trickle about 2 miles up from Bass Camp. It will take most hikers about 6 hours to make a round-trip to the White Canyon-Shinumo Creek confluence. Ambitious hikers may want to explore White Canyon (it has some lovely narrows) or continue up Shinumo Creek to Flint Creek or the Modred Abyss.

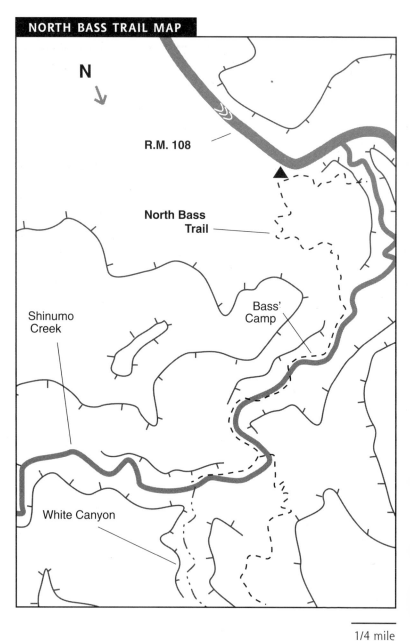

## NORTH BASS TRAIL MAP

N

R.M. 108

North Bass
Trail

Shinumo
Creek

Bass'
Camp

White Canyon

1/4 mile

| | | |
|---|---|---|
| ●●●●●●●●● route | | |
| - - - - - trail | | - - · - - · creekbed |
| ⊤⊤⊤ cliff rim | | ▲ camp |

Upstream view from the North Bass Trail

# Dox Castle

**River Mile:** 108—right
**Time:** 6 to 9 hours
**Difficulty:** Difficult
**Wet or Dry?:** Dry
**Ideal Weather:** Cool
**Potential:** There are limitless hiking options from this route.
**Camp:** Bass or Upper Bass

**Route Description:** A climb to the top of Dox Castle is an experience you'll remember for a lifetime. The route involves lots of steep hiking and climbing, and the views from the top are spectacular.

Before I describe this hike, let me tell you that this route description does not lead to the true summit of Dox Castle. Rather, it leads to a false summit that is about 100 feet lower than the actual summit. Nonetheless, reaching the false summit is a challenging and rewarding journey that will leave most of us really stoked.

Before you start out, procure 120 feet of rope and 12 feet of nylon webbing in order to rappel back down the crux section of this route.

From riverside Bass camp, walk upstream about 250 yards to the first major drainage. This will be the second bouldery wash you come to from camp. At the drainage, boulder hop upstream for about a half mile until you are near the base of the tilted pinkish cliffs of Shinumo Quartzite. From here, turn east and hike up the gully 1,000 vertical feet to the notch in the skyline. At the notch, take a well-deserved rest, because the real climbing is about to begin.

The next 200 yards is mostly a 4th class climb up a jagged ridge, though there are two spots of easy 5th class (5.0-5.2) difficulty. Once on top, stay on the gentle cactus-clustered ridge for 0.25 miles until you are through a distinctive brown ledge. Now make your way around to the southeast side of the castle to the one and only spot where a climb through the yellow and gray Muav Limestone is feasible. When you see a pile of rocks to assist you with the first move you'll know you're at the crux. It is a 5.8 climb over bulging limestone with 15 feet of exposure.

Once above the climb, veer slightly to your right to get through one more minor cliffband, then traverse left for about 150 yards to the base of the final cliffs of Temple Butte Limestone. This last climb is about 100 feet of 4th class that will crest you out on a 7-foot wide ridge looking directly down on Shinumo Creek. From here it is another 100 yards along an exposed and broken ridge to the false summit area 2,440 vertical feet above Bass camp.

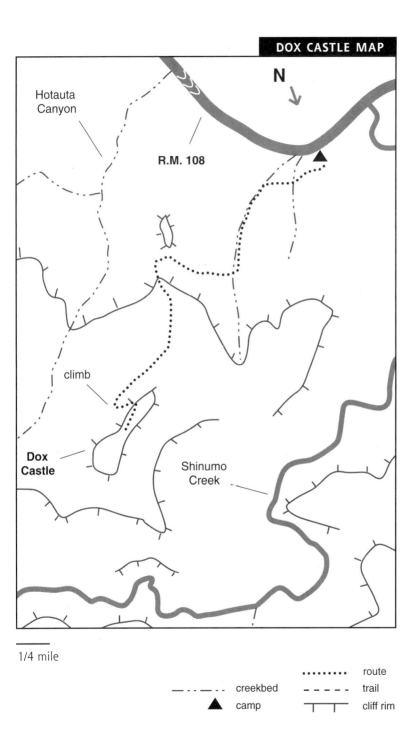

N

Hotauta
Canyon

R.M. 108

climb

Dox
Castle

Shinumo
Creek

1/4 mile

•••••••• route

— · · — · · creekbed        — — — trail

▲ camp        ⊤⊥⊤ cliff rim

Adventurers that make the climb to Dox Castle are rewarded with dizzying views.

# Shinumo Creek

**River Mile:** 108.2 or 108.5—right
**Time:** 3 hours if starting from Bass camp. Thirty minutes to one hour if starting from the mouth of the creek.
**Difficulty:** Moderate from Bass camp. Easy from the creek mouth.
**Ideal Weather:** Hot weather is best for enjoying the waterfall. Any weather is suitable for the hike over from Bass camp.
**Wet or Dry?:** Wet
**Potential:** Shinumo Creek leads upstream for many miles.
**Camp:** A hike up Shinumo Creek is really just a short stop along the river, so any camp is fine.

**Route Description:** There are a few ways to approach a hike at Shinumo Creek. The most common and easiest way is to simply pull in to the mouth of the creek and wade upstream from there. There is a waterfall only 75 yards from the river and most will be content to enjoy the falls and return to the boat. To make more of a hike out of it, some people get dropped off at Bass camp and hike a trail to Shinumo Creek, then re-join their party at the waterfall. This is the same route one would take if he were camped at Bass camp.

From Bass camp, a trail leads uphill from the downstream end of camp. This trail climbs a 200-foot high ridge separating Shinumo Creek from camp. At the top of the ridge there is a wonderful view of the river, Shinumo Creek, the Powell Plateau, and several other features in the area.

Starting down the other side, you'll see Shinumo Creek below. The trail splits when it is about 100 feet above the creek. The right fork continues upstream, gradually descending to the creek in the next 0.3 miles. The left fork drops straight down, descending a 4th class rock face. To get to the river, a 10-foot jump into a pool or a 5.5 boulder downclimb is necessary. Below the falls, there is usually a great swimming hole, but sometimes it fills with gravel making it only knee-deep.

Springtime runoff can make Shinumo Creek too high for this route to be feasible. This usually occurs in April or May. Summer thunderstorm season has its risks too—Shinumo Creek is a big enough drainage to carry huge flash floods.

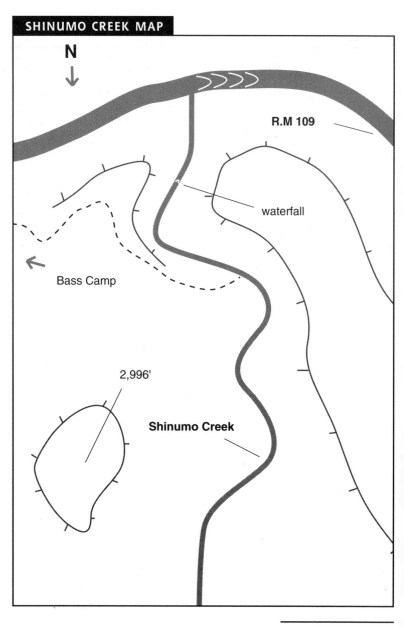

SHINUMO CREEK MAP

N

R.M 109

waterfall

Bass Camp

2,996'

Shinumo Creek

1/4 mile

- · · · · · · · ·  route
- – – – –  trail
- ⊥⊤⊥⊤  cliff rim
- — · · — · ·  creekbed
- ▲  camp

The waterfall on Shinumo Creek is a popular stop for river trips.

# Elves Chasm

**River Mile:** 116.5—left
**Time:** 45 minutes to enjoy the first big waterfall and return.
**Difficulty:** Moderate to the first big waterfall. Difficult to explore farther up the canyon.
**Wet or Dry?:** Wet
**Ideal Weather:** Hot
**Potential:** Six climbs and an exposed walk will have you at an unclimbable amphitheater about 0.5 miles from the river.
**Camp:** There are several camps in the next few miles downstream from Elves. Camping at Elves Chasm is illegal.

**Route Description:** Elves Chasm is a steep boulder-choked canyon filled with clear water, travertine, and stunning greenery. Transparently clear pools ripple from the drip of overhanging springs, and shags of maiden-hair fern cover the cliff walls. Redbud trees grow in such profusion they emulate an Eastern hardwood forest. If ever there was a natural Shangri-La, this is it.

A good destination for most of us is the third distinct waterfall up from the river. To get here, some easy scrambling and boulder hopping is necessary. This 60-foot cascade is a classic Grand Canyon scene as the clear water falls through giant fern-fringed boulders. For those with the desire and climbing ability to explore farther, a route leads up the ledges on creek left.

I could go into great detail about the six major climbs en-route to the top of Elves Chasm, but if you can make it that far, you don't need a guidebook to tell you how to do it. All the climbs are on creek left, some moves are 5th class climbs, and others are 3rd class with big exposure. Plenty of people have fallen here. Don't be a statistic!

The canyon boxes out just beyond a 100-foot trickling waterfall about 0.4 miles from the river. Royal Arch (actually a natural bridge) is located just upstream from the final amphitheater, but it is not attainable from Elves Chasm.

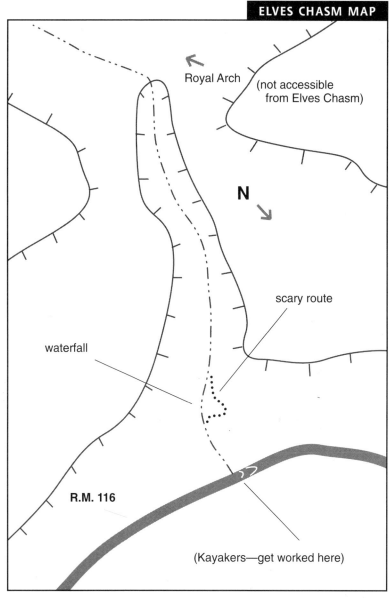

Royal Arch

(not accessible
from Elves Chasm)

N

scary route

waterfall

R.M. 116

(Kayakers—get worked here)

1/4 mile

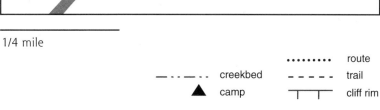

— · · — · ·   creekbed          route

▲   camp          trail

cliff rim

Elves Chasm

# Blacktail Canyon

**River Mile:** 120—right
**Time:** 20 minutes
**Difficulty:** Easy
**Wet or Dry?:** Dry. Two careful scrambles around small pools will keep your feet dry.
**Ideal Weather:** Any
**Potential:** A dedicated hiker could scramble through the Tapeats at the mouth of Blacktail and walk the open creekbed of upper Blacktail for a few miles before getting cliffed out.
**Camp:** There is a big camp at the mouth of Blacktail, downstream of the rapid.

**Route Description:** This is a short hike through pretty Tapeats narrows. It is high on the "instant gratification" meter.

From the beach and big eddy just downstream from Blacktail, hike across the alluvium and enter the creekbed near the river. Head upstream from here along the trickle of clear water that usually dribbles out of the gorge. There are two pools in the creekbed that require either a knee-deep wade or a short scramble to avoid. A chokestone about 0.2 miles up will stop most of us. Sometimes there is a deep pool at the base of this chokestone; other times flash floods fill in the pool with gravel.

If you make the slimy climb beyond the chokestone, you'll find more narrows. It is hardly worth the effort, though; the canyon terminates soon after with another fall.

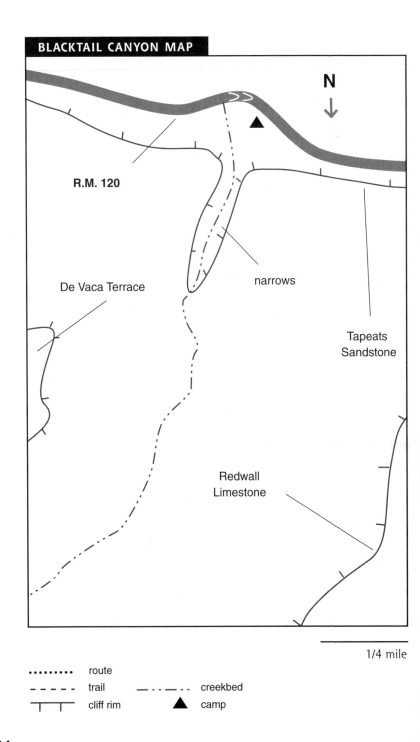

BLACKTAIL CANYON MAP

N

R.M. 120

De Vaca Terrace

narrows

Tapeats
Sandstone

Redwall
Limestone

1/4 mile

•••••••• route

- - - - trail     -··-··- creekbed

⊤⊤⊤ cliff rim     ▲ camp

Tapeats narrows in Blacktail Canyon

# Fossil Canyon

**River Mile:** 125.0—left
**Time:** If starting from the camp below Fossil Rapid on the left, it is 1.5 hours round-trip to the Muav pool, 4 hours round-trip to the "red slide," and 5.5 hours round-trip to the Redwall narrows.
**Difficulty:** Moderate.
**Wet or Dry?:** Dry. The only water in this canyon is a trickle in the Muav and sometimes a muddy pool in the Redwall.
**Ideal Weather:** Cool or Moderate
**Potential:** It is challenging but possible to climb up the creekbed of Fossil to the Esplanade.
**Camp:** The best camp here is 0.5 miles downstream from the canyon mouth on the left, below Fossil Rapid. There is also a big camp at Forster two miles upstream.

**Route Description:** A hike up Fossil Canyon has basically three highlights: pools in Muav Limestone, a unique erosional slope, and Redwall narrows. The Muav pool is about 1 mile up from the river, while the erosional slope and Redwall narrows are 2 and 3 miles up, respectively. As you can see, there are destinations here to suit all energy levels.

The best place to start a hike up Fossil is right above the rapid at the canyon mouth. However, most of you will only be hiking Fossil if you are camped nearby, and the best nearby camp is 0.5 miles downstream from the canyon mouth. If you are camped below Fossil, your hike starts with a sandy 0.5 mile march upstream along the river.

Once in the creekbed of Fossil, there are some Tapeats ledges that make for easy walking initially, but then the footing changes to cobbles and boulders for the remainder of the hike. There is a short appearance of Muav Limestone with one of those patented emerald-green pools making a good rest spot. The next remarkable feature is an area of landslide debris about two miles up. This rare geologic feature is also found on the river at mile 176, where it is known as the Red Slide.

About a mile past Fossil's red slide, the Redwall pinches down on the creek forming a neat narrows. Hiking musicians take note—these Redwall narrows make for incredible acoustics. A pool backed by a smooth slide stopped me, although Harvey Butchart and a few others have slithered up this fall and made it out Fossil Canyon.

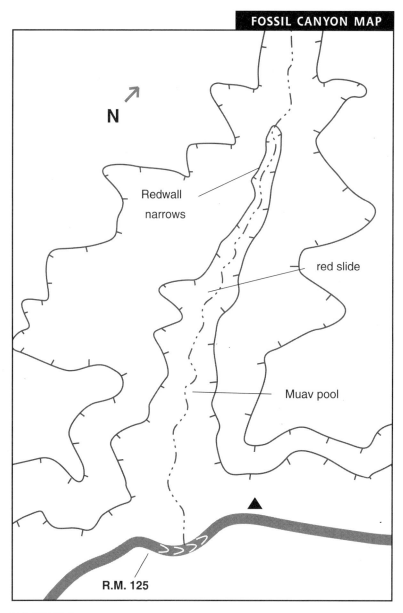

**FOSSIL CANYON MAP**

N

Redwall
narrows

red slide

Muav pool

R.M. 125

1/4 mile

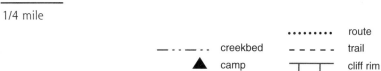

········· route
—·—·—· creekbed    — — — trail
▲ camp            ⊤—⊤ cliff rim

Muav ledges in Fossil Canyon

Palisades of the desert

Swimmimg in the Little Colorado

Hiking along the Nankoweap-Kwagunt saddle

Looking downstream from the granaries

Cruising the top of the Redwall in Marble Gorge

Hucking at Havasu

Glenn Rink rappels Deer Creek Falls

Finding yourself in Grand Canyon

Silver Grotto

Desert hiking

Water in the desert

Waterfall on Stone Creek

Dugald Bremner

Elves Chasm

Hilltop Ruin

En-route to Diamond Peak

Walking through the Muav

# Stone Creek

**River Mile:** 131.9—right
**Time:** 20 minutes to the lower falls and back. Three to four hours to the upper falls and back.
**Difficulty:** Moderate
**Wet or Dry?:** Wet. Though much of this route is on a dry desert trail, there are several creek crossings and lots of inviting water.
**Ideal Weather:** Any. Keep your clothes wet on hot days.
**Potential:** A loop hike up and over into Galloway Canyon is possible here.
**Camp:** Stone Creek has a big camp at the base of Dubendorff Rapid.

**Route Description:** In the summer of 1999, a huge flash flood brought dramatic change to this drainage. The monkey flowers and watercress that provided so many garden-like scenes along the stream's banks are now gone. But nature is defined by change, and Stone Creek will undoubtedly be going through many changes during the first part of the century.

From the big beach below Dubendorff Rapid, a trail leads upstream along Stone Creek to a waterfall at the head of a box canyon. This is about a ten minute walk from the river, and serves as a worthy destination. If you're inspired to see more, return down the trail and look for a cairn indicating the upper trail on creek left. The upper trail traverses two sloping rock faces early, and then it is easy walking. If you lack confidence on unstable footing or are nervous about heights, think twice about this route. No climbing is needed, but there is some exposure.

The trail snakes upstream, weaving along the open canyon. Before the flood of '99, Stone Creek was known for its inviting pools. Lately it is a little different. But hey, that flood debris sure is impressive.

As the canyon of upper Stone closes in, the trail degenerates significantly. Travel gets slower and more difficult, but the scenery coaxes you along with an ever-narrowing canyon. If you go until the canyon boxes out, you'll be treated to a ribbon waterfall sluicing down a mossy slide between narrow canyon walls—an absolutely beautiful place.

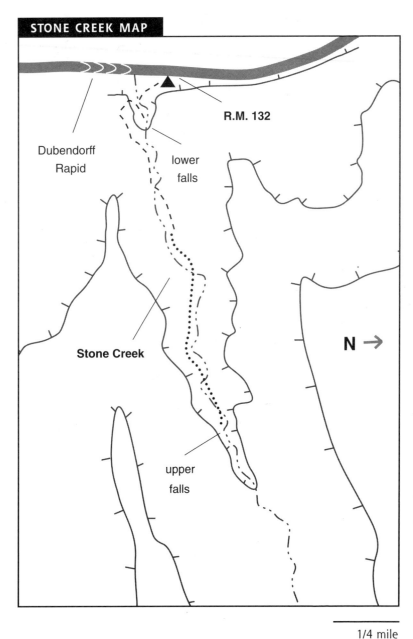

STONE CREEK MAP

Dubendorff
Rapid

R.M. 132

lower
falls

Stone Creek

N →

upper
falls

•••••••• route
– – – – – trail
⊤ ⊤ ⊤ cliff rim

—·—··— creekbed
▲ camp

1/4 mile

Enjoying an idyllic pool on the old Stone Creek

# Thunder River

**River Mile:** 133.7—right
**Time:** 5 hours to Thunder River Springs and back
**Difficulty:** Moderate. The stream crossings are never easy.
**Wet or Dry?:** Wet. If you start the route from the creek-right side of Tapeats Creek and take the creek right trail, you can get to Thunder River with dry feet. The standard route, however, leads across Tapeats Creek three times. Tapeats Creek can be dangerous or even impossible to cross when it is higher than base flow.
**Ideal Weather:** Any
**Potential:** This hike can serve as the first part of the Surprise Valley hike, which goes from Tapeats Creek to Deer Creek. There is also a trail to the North Rim from Thunder River.
**Camp:** Tapeats Camp is at the mouth of Tapeats Creek on creek left. It is a small camp. There is also a camp at the base of the rapid on the right. This camp is bigger, but more exposed. There are also several good camps just downstream from Tapeats Creek.

**Route Description:** A hike to Thunder River is yet another Grand Canyon "classic." Most will find the trail to Thunder River to be quite adventurous, and the destination of this hike—a waterfall called Thunder Springs or Thunder River—is nothing short of spectacular.

From the creek left camp at the mouth of Tapeats Creek, cross the creek to the northwest side (creek right), and pick up the trail that starts up the creek and climbs a steep scree gully. Once you are a couple hundred feet above the creek, the trail starts upstream along the rim of the Tapeats Creek Gorge. In about 0.5 miles, you'll be back along the creek at the head of the gorge. Two hundred yards or so farther upstream the trail splits, giving you two options.

The standard route crosses Tapeats Creek at some picturesque ledges, then stays close to the creek as it winds upstream on creek left. There are a couple short and easy scrambles on this trail before it makes another creek crossing just downstream from the Thunder River confluence. Crossing the creek can be impossible during spring runoff.

The creek right route is harder to follow and farther from the creek. From the trail split just upstream of the gorge, it climbs the creek right slope and takes a meandering but well-cairned course upstream before re-joining the standard route near the confluence with Thunder River.

From the confluence of Tapeats Creek and Thunder River, the trail climbs 1,000 vertical feet in about a mile to the roaring springs of Thunder River. You might encounter backpackers here, as there is a trail leading here from Monument Point—3,800 feet above on the North Rim.

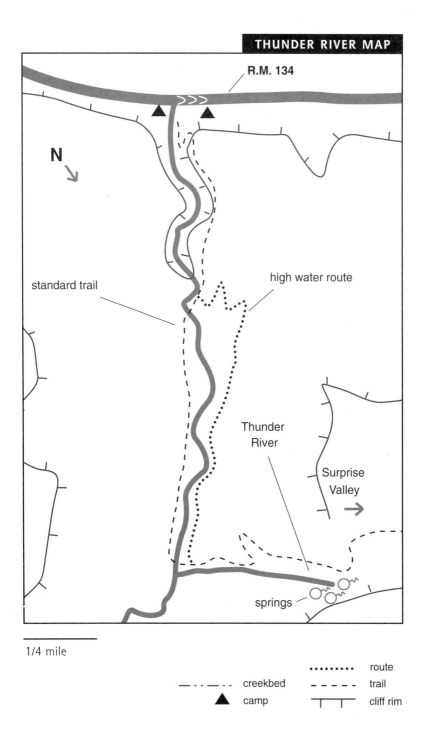

R.M. 134

N

standard trail

high water route

Thunder
River

Surprise
Valley
→

springs

1/4 mile

·—·—·· creekbed    – – – – trail

▲ camp    ⊤⊤ cliff rim

········· route

123

Looking into the Tapeats Creek Gorge

# Surprise Valley

**River Mile:** 133.7 to 136.1—right
**Time:** 5 to 8 hours to go from Tapeats Creek to Deer Creek. Strong hikers could reach Surprise Valley from Deer Creek and return to the river in 3 to 4 hours.
**Difficulty:** Moderate
**Wet or Dry?:** Mostly dry. Surprise Valley itself is dry, but getting there from Tapeats Creek entails some wading.
**Ideal Weather:** Cool or Moderate
**Potential:** Hyper hikers could run to the top of the Redwall on the backpacker's trail.
**Camp:** The best way to see Surprise Valley is with the help of a boat shuttle. Hikers get dropped off at Tapeats Creek and picked up at Deer Creek. At the end of this full day of hiking, you will likely want to camp below Deer Creek. Fortunately, there are several camps here, mostly on river left. It is not permitted to camp on river right at Deer Creek Falls.

**Route Description:** A Surprise Valley hike is a true classic reserved for those who have the time to spend an entire day here. Highlights include Thunder River, a spacious desert valley, Deer Creek Spring, and the Deer Creek narrows. This hike can present some logistical problems, as you begin at Tapeats Creek at mile 134, and finish at Deer Creek, mile 136. This means that a boat shuttle is needed from the gracious non-hikers of the group.

The first stage of this shuttle is getting dropped off at Tapeats Creek. From here, you will cross to creek right, and then pick up a trail that starts up the creek before climbing a scree gully. This trail contours along the rim of the Tapeats Creek Gorge, then leads back to the creek at the head of the gorge. A couple hundred yards farther upstream, the trail splits. The standard trail leads to the right, crosses Tapeats Creek at some ledges just beyond the split, then heads upstream on creek left all the way to the Thunder River confluence. Here you must cross the creek again before making the 1,000-foot ascent to Thunder Springs. For more details on the different routes to Thunder Springs, see the Thunder River description.

A few hundred feet up the trail from Thunder River Springs will bring you to the lip of the Surprise Valley. Following the trail's gradual descent into the bottom of this valley really puts you in the middle of Grand Canyon. The river is far below and the rims are high above. About halfway across the valley, the trail to Monument Point on the North Rim branches off to the right. The way to Deer Creek is straight ahead, moving westward across the desert.

The trail gradually exits the open country of the valley, leading down a drainage toward cottonwood-lined Deer Creek. Before you strike off for the patio of Deer Creek, a nice stop can be made at Deer Creek Spring—a smaller version of Thunder River Spring that has plenty of shade and a hiker-manipulated sitting area known as the "Throne Room."

After resting at the Throne Room, continue down to the peaceful Deer Creek Patio, where you'll likely see other Canyon visitors. From here it is a short trail walk above the Deer Creek narrows (acrophobiacs will not like this part) and back to the river at Deer Creek Falls, a fitting grand finale to a great hike.

Thunder River is a highlight of the Surprise Valley hike.

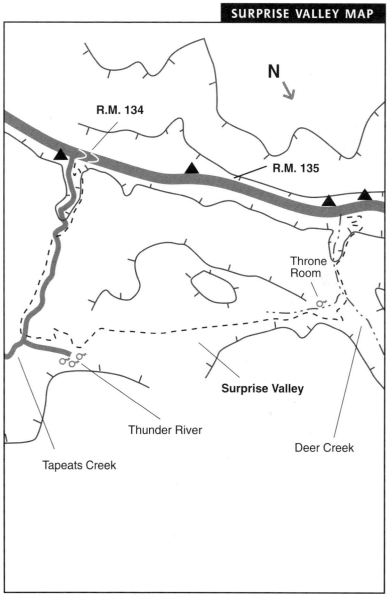

N

R.M. 134

R.M. 135

Throne
Room

Surprise Valley

Thunder River

Deer Creek

Tapeats Creek

1/4 mile

............ route

—··—··— creekbed

▲ camp

- - - - - trail

⊤──⊤ cliff rim

# Deer Creek

**River Mile:** 136.1—right
**Time:** 1 hour, 30 minutes to go to the patio and back. (This is only 40 minutes hiking time, but you'll want to spend a few minutes hanging out at the patio.)
**Difficulty:** Easy to Moderate. There is a trail the entire way, but it has some elevation gain and acrophobiacs will be challenged while hiking along a ledge above the Deer Creek narrows.
**Wet or Dry?:** Dry. This hike is not long, and there is a cool clear creek at the turnaround spot, so many do it in river sandals.
**Ideal Weather:** Any
**Potential:** There is a trail leading from Deer Creek to the North Rim.
**Camp:** There are several large camps just downstream on the left. Camping is illegal at the mouth of Deer Creek.

**Route Description:** Powell's entry reads: "Just after dinner we pass a stream on the right, which leaps into the Colorado by a direct fall of more than 100 feet, forming a beautiful cascade...But we have little time to spend in admiration; so on we go." Had our explorers hiked to upper Deer Creek, they would have found scenery as peaceful as the waterfall is majestic.

Upstream from the falls, Deer Creek runs perfectly down the middle of a rock amphitheater about as soothing as any natural setting can be. Cottonwoods throw shade onto sidewalks of Tapeats Sandstone that border the creek. Bright green watercress crowds the edges of the swift, clear stream. It is a great place for meditation, or a nap. You will likely have to share this spot with backpackers or other river runners. Everyone wants to see Grand Canyon's most beautiful places, and this is one of them.

To get to this peaceful patio, take the trail beginning on the downstream side of Deer Creek Falls. This trail switchbacks uphill; first through vegetation (watch out for the poison ivy) then across open desert. There is some 3rd class scrambling on the route. The trail stops its climb at a river overlook beside the top of the falls. From here, you'll wind along a ledge above the Deer Creek narrows—a spectacular incised gorge in the Tapeats Sandstone. Don't get too curious peering into the narrows, an extrication from the narrows would be difficult and expensive. Assuming, of course, that the fall didn't kill you.

You will notice the narrows relenting shortly before you arrive at the patio. Upstream from the patio, there are backpacker's campsites and plenty of cottonwoods to find shade under. There once were even more big cottonwoods than there are today, but a fire started by a backpacker burning his toilet paper charred about 60 acres along the creek in 1994.

Energetic types can proceed up to Deer Spring—a waterfall pouring right out of the cliff. Just continue up the trail that runs along the west side of Deer Creek to where it fords the creek about 0.5 miles from the patio. After crossing the creek, the trail climbs uphill to the east, heading for Surprise Valley and Tapeats Creek. In about 0.3 miles, you can take a spur trail over to the waterfall and the "Throne Room"—an area of man-made rock thrones adjacent to the spring that is a great place to hang out.

Relaxing along Deer Creek

Lisa Gelczis

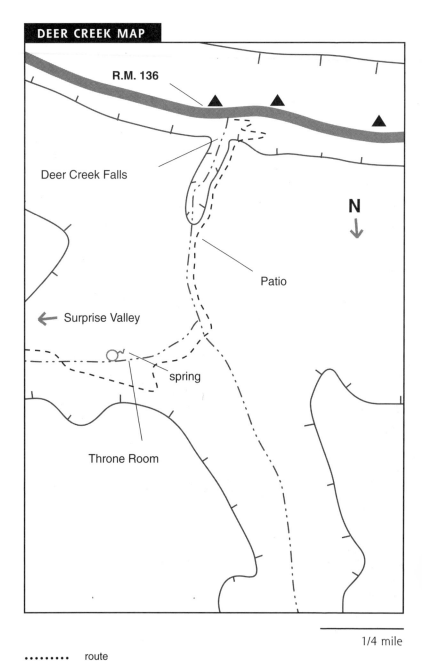

# DEER CREEK MAP

R.M. 136

Deer Creek Falls

N

Patio

← Surprise Valley

spring

Throne Room

1/4 mile

......... route
- - - - trail        -·-·-· creekbed
⊤⊤⊤ cliff rim        ▲ camp

Upstream view from the Deer Creek Trail

# Kanab Creek

**River Mile:** 143.4—right
**Time:** 2 to 3 hours to get to the "overhanging curve" and back
**Difficulty:** Moderate.
**Wet or Dry?:** Wet
**Ideal Weather:** Moderate or Hot
**Potential:** The Kanab Creek drainage has a lifetime of hiking in it.
**Camp:** There is a small to medium camp on the upstream side of Kanab Creek, and there are several big camps between Deer Creek and 140 mile.

**Route Description:** Kanab is a massive drainage. Its waters gather in the juniper hills above the town of Kanab, Utah, fifty air miles away. From the air, Kanab Creek is so sinuous and deep that it is sometimes confused with Marble Gorge to the east.

Walking along the bottom of this chasm is a quintessential Grand Canyon experience. A clear stream accordians between pools and tumbling cascades. Redwall cliffs stretch upward more high and sheer than anywhere else in the Canyon. There is no trail here. Nature's floods take care of any path that develops in the gravel creekbed. The footing in the creek is sometimes gravel, sometimes mud. Shortcuts around deep pools will take you over rounded boulders and across sidewalk terraces of limestone.

At least two hours of hiking here are needed to get the feel of the place. The sights get more spectacular the farther one gets from the river. A giant curving overhang of Muav Limestone about 2 miles up makes a nice turnaround spot.

If you have the time, explore as far as you can up the main creekbed, or check out one of the side canyons that enter Kanab Creek. Kanab is full of surprises.

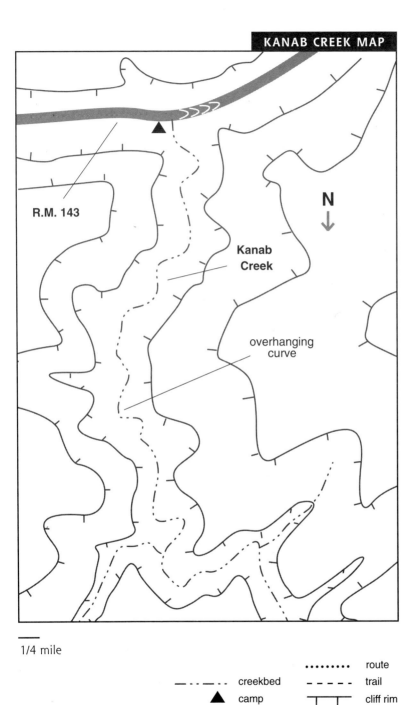

R.M. 143

Kanab
Creek

overhanging
curve

N

1/4 mile

- · - · - creekbed
▲ camp

········· route
- - - - trail
┬┬┬┬ cliff rim

Many beautiful pools dot the course of Kanab Creek.

# Olo Canyon

**River Mile:** 145.5—left
**Time:** An hour for a small group to go past the first pool and back
**Difficulty:** Difficult. A rope climb is needed to enter the canyon, and lots of climbing and scrambling is needed to proceed.
**Wet or Dry?:** Wet
**Ideal Weather:** Hot
**Potential:** I have not heard of any routes out of Olo, but a good climber might find one.
**Camp:** There is a small camp at the mouth of Olo, but it vanishes periodically from flash floods.

**Route Description:** Olo is a challenging and spectacular canyon to explore. It makes a dramatic dive through smooth Muav Limestone before surrendering its narrow chambers to the gorge of the Colorado. For those willing to make the difficult entrance to this canyon, rewarding scenery awaits.

To enter the canyon, you'll have to climb a free-hanging rope that dangles next to a modest waterfall at the mouth of Olo. This is no easy task. The rope tends to spin as it is weighted and the water falling from above pays no heed to the climber's struggle. The last time I was here, the rope had been improved to a rope ladder, making the climb into the canyon easier than before, but still difficult.

There is also a climbing route just downstream from the mouth. It is a tricky traverse across rotten rock. I wish I could tell you the difficulty of this climb, but it was such a scary experience I've repressed it from my memory.

Once at the top of the rope, you'll be greeted by a pool and a 5.1 climb around it on polished limestone. Above here, Olo opens into a lovely amphitheater backed by a travertine fall. This is a logical turnaround spot, as downclimbing the travertine fall is even dicier than climbing the rope at the mouth of the canyon.

If you are a climber and decide to go beyond the travertine fall (5.2, 20-foot exposure), you'll find more gorgeous pools sandwiched between walls of polished Muav Limestone. About 1 mile up from the river, the water disappears and the canyon opens a bit, allowing acacias to grow.

On the return trip, I like to carefully jump into both pools at the mouth of the canyon if they have been flushed out recently. The pool above the rope is usually deep and clear. The big pool below the rope at the mouth has always been deep for me—I've never hit bottom. However, flash floods periodically fill the pool with gravel and boulders, so it's best to have someone swim around and see how deep it is before you jump. Good luck!

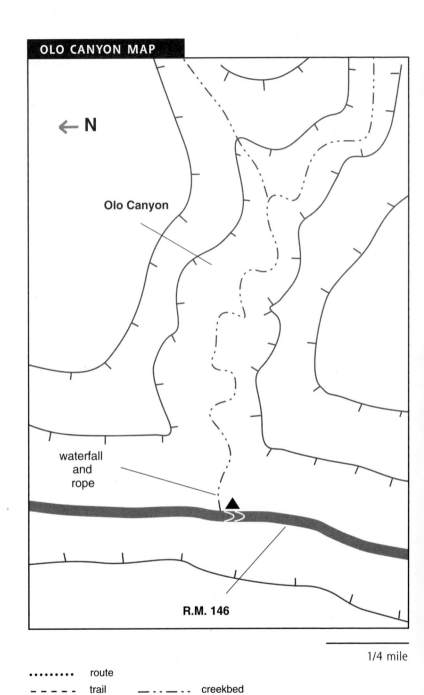

OLO CANYON MAP

← N

Olo Canyon

waterfall
and
rope

R.M. 146

1/4 mile

......... route
- - - - - trail          -··-··- creekbed
⊤ ⊤ cliff rim         ▲ camp

The rope at the mouth of Olo

# Matkatamiba

**River Mile:** 148—left
**Time:** 30 minutes
**Difficulty:** Easy to Moderate. This is a short hike that requires one little scramble and walking along a narrow ledge trail.
**Wet or Dry?:** Wet
**Ideal Weather:** Moderate or Hot
**Potential:** With some climbing, there are routes to the Esplanade from upper Matkatamiba Canyon.
**Camp:** There is a medium-sized camp directly across from the mouth of Matkat. Kanab Creek has a small camp 4.5 miles upstream. "Matkat Hotel" is 0.4 miles downstream, on the left.

**Route Description:** Matkatamiba is one of the most-visited side canyons in Grand Canyon, and for good reason. Narrow serpentine walls of Muav Limestone encase a small clear stream near the mouth, and a wonderful limestone amphitheater lies a short way upstream.

About 50 yards from the mouth of Matkat, most will want to detour out of the narrowing canyon bottom and walk up ledges on creek left to a narrow trail. Less agile people might need a boost out of the creek bottom and onto the ledges, but from there it is simply careful walking to the patio—an area of broad polished ledges at the head of the narrows.

Adventurous types will want to return to the river via the narrows. It is fun to try and chimney your way between the walls and keep your feet dry, but most of us will end up wading at least once.

Boat parking can be difficult at Matkatamiba. During the busy summer months, it is a good idea to pull over on river right at the spring upstream from Matkat and scout out your landing zone.

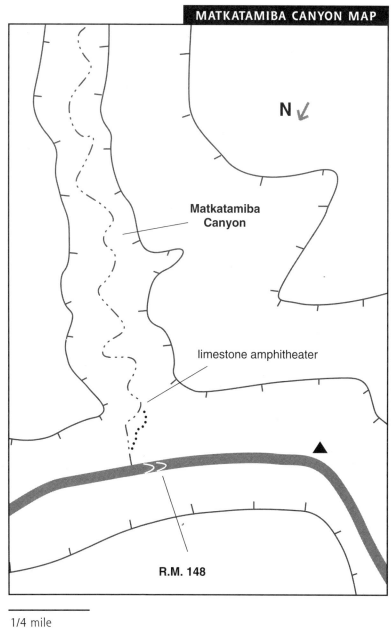

N

Matkatamiba
Canyon

limestone amphitheater

R.M. 148

1/4 mile

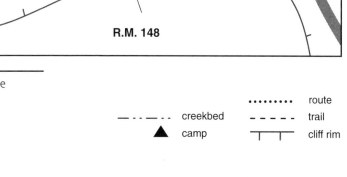

········· route

—·—·—·· creekbed

– – – – trail

▲ camp

⊤—⊤ cliff rim

Stemming in Matkat

# 150 Mile Canyon

**River Mile:** 149.7—right
**Time:** 15 minutes
**Difficulty:** Easy to the first chokestone. Difficult to go farther.
**Wet or Dry?:** Dry. A few small pools are easily avoided.
**Ideal Weather:** Any
**Potential:** An overhanging chokestone stops progress a quarter mile from the river.
**Camp:** "Matkat Hotel" is about a mile upstream on the left. "Upset Hotel" is 0.5 miles below the rapid, on the left. Both are fine camps.

**Route Description:** This is the canyon at Upset Rapid. A short scramble up 150 Mile Canyon isn't much of a hike, but since you will likely be stopped here to scout the rapid anyway, you might as well check out the canyon.

The first major hindrance in 150 Mile Canyon is a chokestone about 150 yards from the river. A rugged scramble on the creek left side of this chokestone will get you up to the next level where you'll find a second chokestone. A 5th class climb up the wall on creek right will have you above this second wedged boulder where you will encounter—you guessed it—another chokestone. This third fall will turn back even good climbers, so relax and enjoy the scenic limestone narrows.

Upset Rapid was named on the 1923 USGS trip when Emery Kolb flipped here. The rapid is much more difficult at low water than it is at higher flows, when the formidable hole at the bottom washes out.

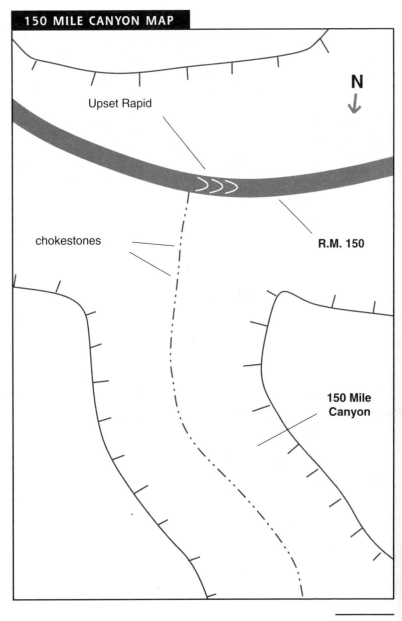

Upset Rapid

chokestones

R.M. 150

150 Mile
Canyon

N

1/4 mile

......... route
– – – – trail        – · – · – · creekbed
⊤⊤⊤ cliff rim        ▲ camp

142

Muav narrows in 150 Mile Canyon

# Havasu

~~~~~~~~~~

**River Mile:** 156.8—left
**Time:** 4 to 6 hours to go to Beaver Falls and back
**Difficulty:** Moderate. Be careful at the stream crossings.
**Wet or Dry?:** Wet
**Ideal Weather:** Hot
**Potential:** Spectacular Mooney Falls is about six miles upstream. The village of Supai is eight miles up.
**Camp:** Camping is not allowed at the mouth of Havasu. There are several small ledge camps on river left within three miles upstream from Havasu. "Matkat Hotel," "Upset Hotel," and Ledges are popular camps between miles 148 and 152.

**Route Description:** On summer afternoons, the mouth of Havasu Creek can be so jammed full of boats and people it prompts many to call it "Havazoo." Naturally, there is a reason for this popularity: Havasu is a bitchin' place.

A flourishing stream of turquoise-blue water spills over travertine ledges and quietly rests in inviting pools. Cottonwood trees provide quenching shade for those who want to sit and watch nature drift by, and a fantasy-land trail leads upstream for those who need to explore.

The trail starts just downstream from the mouth of the canyon on Muav ledges that are noticeably worn from foot traffic. From here it leads upstream as a well-beaten path, but it is not long before you'll be wading across the creek (it can be deep and swift) in search of the best walking route. Because of the heavy amount of foot traffic here, trails are usually evident. However, flash floods periodically tear through and eliminate man's handiwork. Havasu is a huge drainage that carries big floods. Be aware.

If you continue far, the trail will lead across the creek a few times, climb up bluffs adjacent to the stream, and even lead through a travertine tunnel. It is somewhat of a "magical mystery tour," as the Fab Four might say.

A popular destination is Beaver Falls—a stair-stepping cascade three miles from the river with some great swimming holes. Just before Beaver Canyon enters on creek left and Havasu Creek takes a turn to the southeast, look for cairns leading up the creek right ledges. After traversing high above Havasu Creek, a spur trail will lead down to upper Beaver Falls. Some choose to return via the creek bottom from here. Beaver is the last of four major waterfalls on Havasu Creek. The next one upstream is Mooney Falls: a booming vertical drop of over 100 feet.

To get to Mooney, you must continue upstream from Beaver Falls at a quick pace. It is a long day to float to Havasu, hike to Mooney, return to the river, and then go find camp.

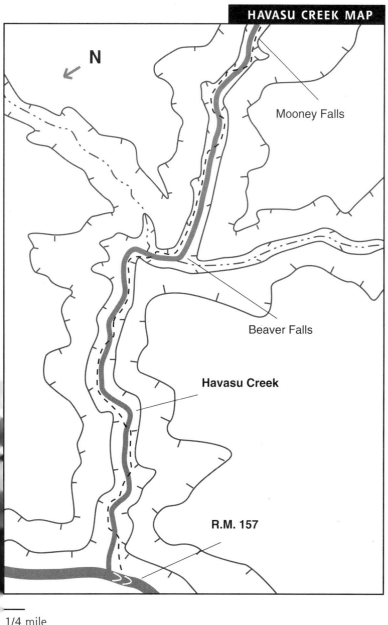

N

Mooney Falls

Beaver Falls

**Havasu Creek**

**R.M. 157**

1/4 mile

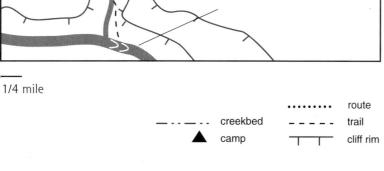

•••••••••  route

—··—··—·  creekbed          — — — —  trail

▲  camp          ┬──┬  cliff rim

Mooney Falls on Havasu Creek

# Tuckup Canyon

**River Mile:** 164.4—right
**Time:** 1 hour
**Difficulty:** Difficult. A 5.3 climb with exposure is necessary to do the standard hike.
**Wet or Dry?:** Dry. The few pools can be avoided.
**Ideal Weather:** Any
**Potential:** An all-day hike can lead to the wide-open country of the Esplanade, or even the rim.
**Camp:** There is a big camp at the mouth of Tuckup.

**Route Description:** If you've decided to bypass Havasu, but you still want a good hike in this part of the Muav gorge, Tuckup Canyon offers a wealth of exploration options.

Once past a sharp, fresh rockfall, Tuckup has easy walking in Muav narrows, but a fall stops progress about 0.3 miles from the river. To get around this fall, retreat 100 yards and climb up an exposed face of limestone on creek right. There is a nail in the rock here that leaders may want to use as an anchor for others. This climb will weed out the non-climbers with its 5.3 difficulty and moderate exposure. Once about 75 feet above the creekbed, this climb intersects a trail that contours upstream and back into the creek bottom. This is the most beautiful part of Tuckup Canyon. Gorgeous sapphire-tinged pools nestle in the Muav Limestone, and Redwall cliffs tower above. For a standard hour-long hike in Tuckup, enjoy this Eden, and then return the way you came.

For those who wish to continue upstream, another route on creek right leads across a slope of travertine at the next major falls. With a few scrambles, hikers can make it all the way out Tuckup Canyon to the Esplanade— the spacious country at the top of the Supai formation. From the Esplanade, routes through the remaining layers to the rim of Grand Canyon are abundant. If you want to make it to the Esplanade and back, plan on a full day.

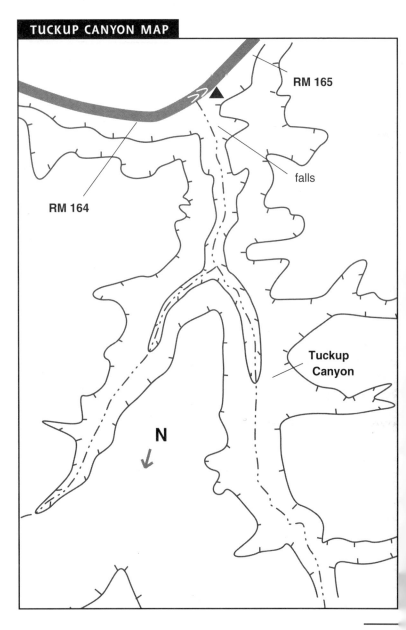

## TUCKUP CANYON MAP

RM 165

RM 164

falls

Tuckup
Canyon

N

1/4 mile

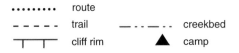

········· route
– – – – – trail          —·—·—·— creekbed
⊤⊤⊤⊤ cliff rim          ▲ camp

A Redwall arch in Tuckup Canyon

# National Canyon

**River Mile:** 166.4—left
**Time:** 4 hours to the big chokestones and back
**Difficulty:** Difficult. This is no place for acrophobiacs.
**Wet or Dry?:** Wet
**Ideal Weather:** Moderate
**Potential:** With a few difficulties, you can hike out to the rim here, although it would take a full day to get there.
**Camp:** There are two big beautiful camps at National.

**Route Description:** National Canyon is spectacular. A tiny creek gurgles through narrows of Muav Limestone while huge Redwall faces stand guard a thousand feet overhead. If you are not a climber, a hike to the lower narrows is well worth the effort. If you are comfortable with heights, National is a place where you'll want to spend some quality time.

The first water surfaces about 0.3 miles from the beach. There is a recent rockfall to avoid just upstream from here, but mostly you'll enjoy easy walking on flat ledges and creek gravels. About 0.5 miles up from the river is the mouth of the lower narrows. If you don't have lots of time for exploration, scramble up the creekbed here and enjoy the narrows. To go up the canyon farther, look for a route on creek left, just at the mouth of the narrows.

The first move on the route is 5th class, but with negligible exposure. Farther up, the climbing is 4th class, but a fall will send you plunging 50 feet to the creekbed below. Follow the cairns along the ledges and the route will lead back to the creekbed.

Once back in the creek, you'll be dancing across limestone shelves and wading through crystal clear pools on your way upstream. The next major obstacle is about 0.4 miles farther, where two chokestones block the narrows. Both of these chokestones require 5th class bouldering to surmount. Above the chokestones, the canyon's character changes slightly as huge boulders fill the widening creekbed and the water sinks into the gravels underfoot.

Unless you have a full day to explore National, you'd better turn around here, where the water disappears. The canyon's character stays the same until above the Redwall, where the terrain opens and there are routes to the rim.

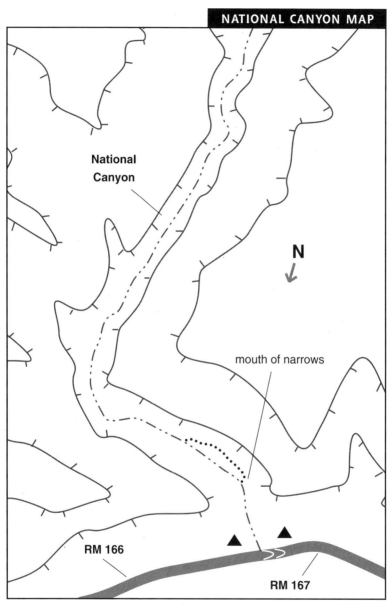

National
Canyon

N

mouth of narrows

RM 166

RM 167

1/4 mile

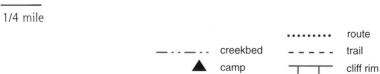

—··—··— creekbed     •••••••• route
▲ camp              — — — trail
                    ⊤—⊤ cliff rim

Waterslides in National Canyon

# Fern Glen Canyon

**River Mile:** 168.0—right
**Time:** 45 minutes
**Difficulty:** Moderate
**Wet or Dry?:** Dry
**Ideal Weather:** Any
**Potential:** A travertine fall blocks sane progress 0.5 miles from the river. Truly intrepid explorers have climbed this fall.
**Camp:** There is a huge beach for camping at Fern Glen.

**Route Description:** Fern Glen is located in one of the more spectacular sections of Grand Canyon. Gigantic cliffs of Redwall and Muav Limestone stoically loom over the river, and chunks of burnt-red Supai Sandstone are visible through gaps in the rims. Equally dramatic as the main river gorge are the many side canyons near here: Havasu, Tuckup, National, Mohawk, Fern Glen. Each of these canyons has something unique, yet they all share common qualities. Fern Glen Canyon is the easiest place to view these common traits with a short hike.

Five minutes of walking from the beach will have you in the shade of converging limestone walls. At the head of the narrows, an emerald pool hides from the sun beside a house-sized boulder. A short 4th class scramble will have you onto the next level, where a wall draped in maidenhair fern awaits. Another scramble around a pool will reveal more ferns, along with other rich and lustrous growth dripping out of the wall. A trickling travertine fall seals the back of the room. There is no way to go farther, nor is there a need.

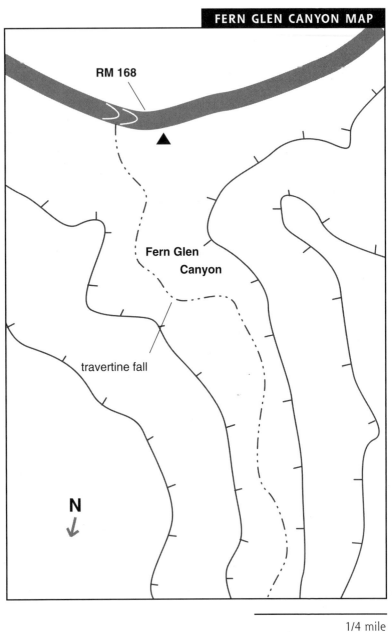

RM 168

Fern Glen
Canyon

travertine fall

N

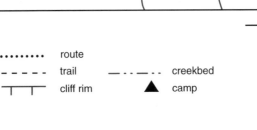

········· route
- - - - - trail          —··—··— creekbed
┬─┬─┬─ cliff rim          ▲ camp

1/4 mile

154

Fern Glen Canyon

# Mohawk Canyon

**River Mile:** 171.5—left
**Time:** 1 hour, 45 minutes to the travertine springs and back
**Difficulty:** Moderate
**Wet or Dry?:** Dry. There is a small amount of water here, but it is easily avoided.
**Ideal Weather:** Cool or Moderate
**Potential:** With some route finding, you can make it to the rim here.
**Camp:** There are two big camps at the mouth of Mohawk. One is above the rapid, one is below.

**Route Description:** From its mouth, Mohawk Canyon doesn't look like much. The cobble creekbed and wide-set canyon walls are less than intriguing when compared to the other narrow and inviting canyons along this stretch of river. It wasn't until I found myself camped here that I finally took an obligatory walk up this overlooked canyon. I was pleasantly surprised. Mohawk Canyon gets neater the farther you go. In fact, Mohawk's most scenic sections are likely beyond the lower two miles that I have seen.

Things start dry and open. Shade is scarce, and the rocks are of a perfectly imperfect size—too big to lay flat and too small to be stable boulders. Be diligent, your perseverance will begin to pay off about 20 minutes from the river, when water begins to emerge from the creek's gravels. Bedrock starts to replace the alluvium, and seeps give life to water-loving green plants.

The canyon continually changes, teasing you along. The walking is never easy, but neither is it ever too difficult. From time to time, you will have to do some boulder hopping and scrambling up bedrock ledges.

A redbud tree signals the proximity of a multitude of seeps. Cattails, willows, and ferns crowd a moist travertine slope where water runs down a rocky shelf in thin glistening sheets. These travertine springs serve as a good turnaround point unless you have several hours to explore.

Upstream, the canyon gets boulder-choked and begins to narrow before opening up again. Beyond this, it looks interesting, but I can't say I've been lucky enough to see it.

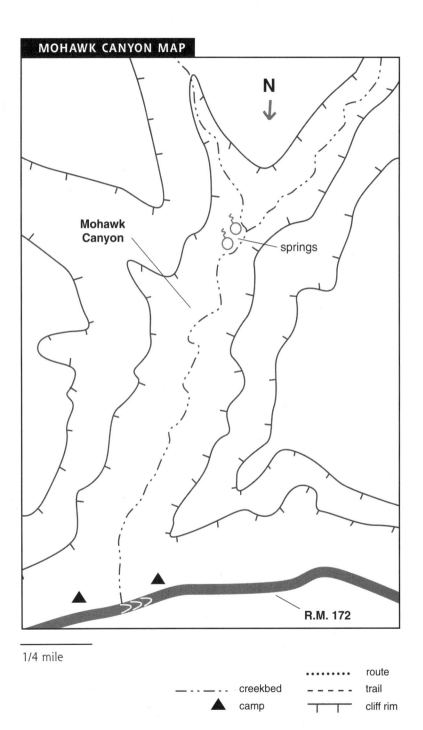

MOHAWK CANYON MAP

N

Mohawk
Canyon

springs

R.M. 172

1/4 mile

creekbed · · · · · · · · · · route
camp — — — trail
cliff rim

Walking near the springs in Mohawk Canyon

# Vulcans Throne

**River Mile:** 179.0—right
**Time:** 7 to 10 hours to the top of Vulcans Throne and back, and at least 2.5 hours to the road at the top of the gorge and back.
**Difficulty:** Moderate to Difficult. There is no climbing, but this is a long uphill hike on loose rock.
**Wet or Dry?:** Dry
**Ideal Weather:** Cool. This is one of the hottest places on earth in summer.
**Potential:** The summit of Vulcans Throne is the most interesting objective in the area.
**Camp:** The big beach below Lava and the camp above the left scout spot are both good access points for this hike.

**Route Description:** There are two hiking options here: long and very long. A hike up the Lava Falls Trail to the road is plenty rewarding and gets you out of the Canyon and into expansive sagebrush country. From here, Vulcans Throne looms as a tempting goal. At the summit of this cinder cone, you'll be treated to a broad view of the Arizona Strip, the Kaibab Plateau, and the vast western Grand Canyon. If you are feeling claustrophobic and energetic, this is the hike for you. A grueling 3.5 miles and 3400 vertical feet will have you out of the Canyon and on a mountaintop in big sky country.

To find the Lava Falls Trail: From the boat tie-up spot for the right scout at Lava, head upstream 150 yards where you'll see a flurry of cairns. The trail begins its climb here. It is a cairned and beaten path all the way to the top.

The trail goes up a steep, rocky, loose gully before making it to a more stable creosote-covered hillside. Just below the rim, the trail switchbacks through basalt rimrock and finally tops out at a dirt road. Sometimes there are automobiles here.

To summit Vulcans Throne, continue your plod up the commanding cinder cone. The ascent is slow due to the soft cinders underfoot. For every step gained, a half step is lost. Just as you finally crest the summit, a second dome is revealed that is slightly higher than the one you are standing on! Thankfully, a ridge connects the two summits, and a quick and easy walk will have you on the higher one.

Despite the tedious challenges, a hike to the top is tremendously rewarding. This is one of my very favorite Grand Canyon hikes.

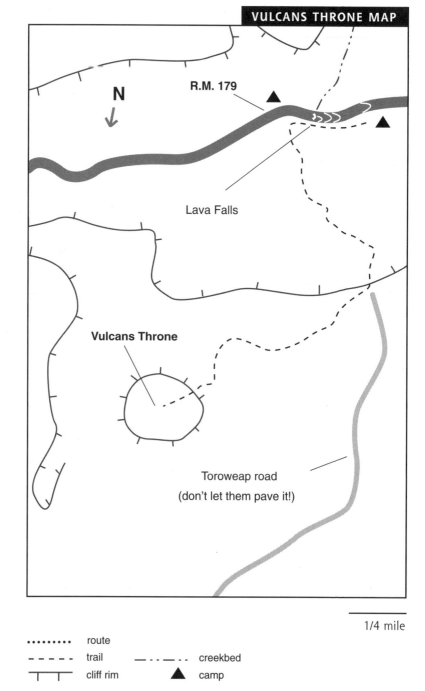

VULCANS THRONE MAP

N

R.M. 179

Lava Falls

Vulcans Throne

Toroweap road
(don't let them pave it!)

1/4 mile

•••••••• route

– – – – trail       –  ·  –  ·  – creekbed

⊤  ⊤  ⊤ cliff rim       ▲ camp

Vulcans Throne as seen from Prospect Canyon

# Prospect Canyon

**River Mile:** 179.2—left
**Time:** 2.5 hours to the base of the scree and back
**Difficulty:** Moderate to the base of the scree, with lots of boulder hopping and a scramble or two. Difficult if you go for the rim, with lots of steep hiking on loose rock. Careful route selection and foot placement is essential.
**Wet or Dry?:** Dry
**Ideal Weather:** Cool or Moderate
**Potential:** About 3 hours of desert mountaineering will have you on the rim in the expansive Prospect Valley.
**Camp:** Above Lava on the left is a medium-sized camp that accesses this hike. Kayaks, duckies, and canoes could reach this hike from the Lower Lava (Tequila Beach) camp by carrying upstream and ferrying across the river just below Lava Falls.

**Route Description:** Though hiking isn't generally the first thing on boater's minds above Lava Falls, Prospect Canyon is here if you are so inclined. A hike up Prospect offers views of Vulcans Throne and the lava flow across the river. Unexpectedly, there are also a couple of small pools and some monkey flowers in Prospect. For gnarly hikers, Prospect can also serve as a route to the rim.

This is the drainage that is responsible for Grand Canyon's biggest rapid—Lava Falls. A hike up Prospect illustrates the ephemeral nature of the geology here. Debris-flows come down Prospect and change Lava Falls periodically. Maybe the next big debris-flow will make Lava a perennial class V?

From the mouth of Prospect Canyon (on the left at Lava Falls), head up the steep and bouldery debris-flow bed. Travel is slow, as you will be either boulder hopping or scrambling the entire way. When the boulders of the creekbed stop at the base of a long scree gully, you are at the standard turnaround spot. Views here reveal the distant river and Vulcans Throne—the conical cinder cone on the north side of the gorge.

Anyone going for the rim via Prospect Canyon should proceed slowly and carefully. The hiking is similar to mountaineering, with unstable footing, steep slopes, and prevalent rockfall. Even gusts of wind seem to trigger rockslides in this geologically-active area. The scree slope leading to the rim is littered with loose rocks of varying sizes, and one slip could send you on a slide-for-life. There are a couple of different route options near the top. I worked my way left as I climbed and had a 4th class climb through the basalt near the rim.

At the top, expansive views across open country are your reward. The rounded domes of Mt. Emma (7702 feet) and her companions are a fresh sight after weeks of vertical cliffs in the canyon.

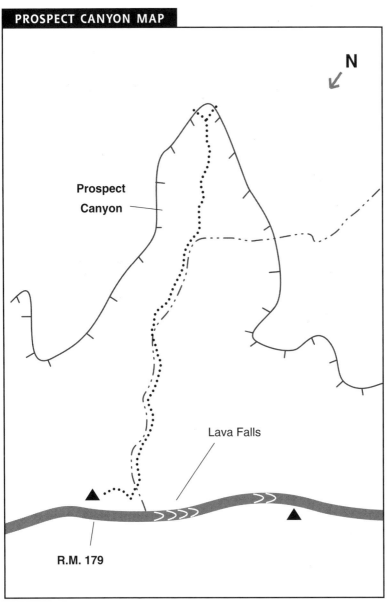

## PROSPECT CANYON MAP

N

Prospect
Canyon

Lava Falls

R.M. 179

1/4 mile

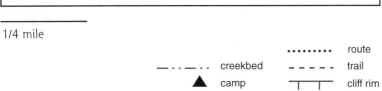

creekbed            route

camp            trail

cliff rim

The far-left scout at Lava

# Parashant Canyon

**River Mile:** 198.5—right
**Time:** 1 hour, 45 minutes to the first narrows and back
**Difficulty:** Easy. This is a relatively flat creekbed hike.
**Wet or Dry?:** Dry
**Ideal Weather:** Cool
**Potential:** All day. The Redwall narrows are 7 miles up from the river.
**Camp:** There is a large and shady camp at the mouth of Parashant.

**Route Description:** Parashant is a huge drainage in the western Canyon. It is not uncommon for floods of 1,000 cfs or more to come roaring down its wide riverbed after heavy thunderstorms. The canyon is somewhat open and meandering in the lower end, with beaches of mesquite trees trimming the dry wash. The canyon does get moderately narrow about a mile up from the river, but then opens up again for several miles.

I have only been up the lower few miles of Parashant, but I'm told that there are beautiful Redwall narrows 7 miles up from the river. With a little route-finding and climbing, there are also several places to get up to the Esplanade from Parashant Wash.

By Grand Canyon standards, this is not a place that offers instant breathtaking beauty. However, for someone with a strong desire to explore, Parashant is an artery running to the heart of big wild country.

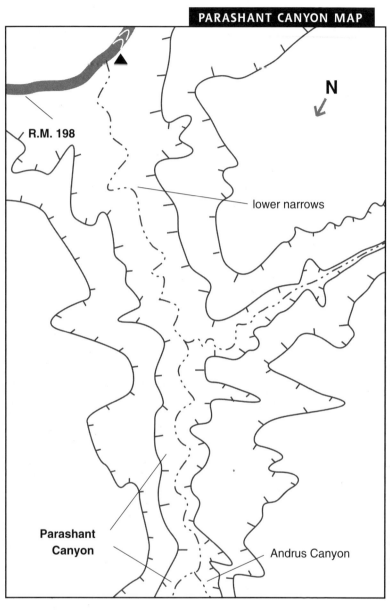

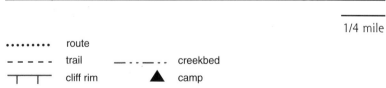

PARASHANT CANYON MAP

N

R.M. 198

lower narrows

Parashant
Canyon

Andrus Canyon

1/4 mile

•••••••• route
– – – – – trail          – · – · – · – creekbed
⊤⊤⊤⊤ cliff rim          ▲ camp

The wide riverbed of Parashant Canyon can carry big floods.

# Fall Canyon

**River Mile:** 211.5—right
**Time:** 1 hour, 30 minutes to the Redwall fall and back
**Difficulty:** Easy to Moderate. Most of the route requires boulder hopping.
**Wet or Dry?:** Dry
**Ideal Weather:** Cool
**Potential:** A Redwall fall stops progress about a mile from the river.
**Camp:** A large camp is located on the upstream side of Fall Canyon's mouth.

**Route Description:** Fall Canyon is in an obscure part of the Canyon: too far from Diamond Creek to serve as a good last night's camp, but below most of the major attractions of the lower end. Because of its awkward location, Fall Canyon remains a quiet and seldom-visited spot. If you happen to be seeking unspoiled quiet, this could be the perfect place.

The bottom of Fall Canyon is mostly littered with table-sized boulders. Occasionally, the creekbed is graced with the gorgeous moss-green shale of the Bright Angel formation. These soft olive shales stack together in an organized stratigraphy, giving intricate beauty to a vast place.

The first fall in the canyon has a route around it on creek left. The second major fall is a 200-foot drop in the Redwall. This is the turnaround point.

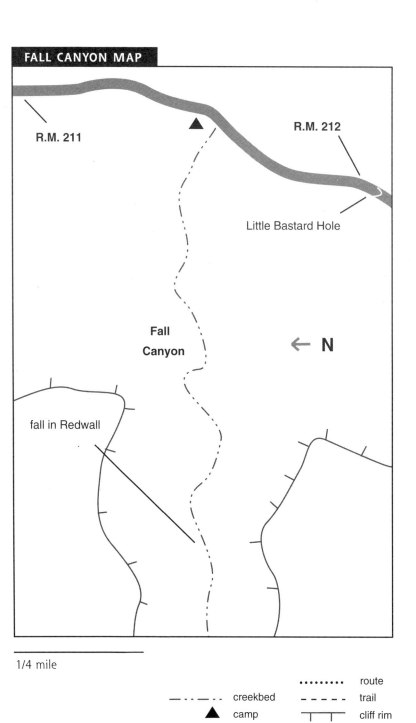

FALL CANYON MAP

R.M. 211

R.M. 212

Little Bastard Hole

Fall
Canyon

← N

fall in Redwall

1/4 mile

.......... route
−·−·−· creekbed      − − − − trail
▲ camp               ⊤ ⊤ cliff rim

Lovely ledges in Fall Canyon

# 220 Mile Canyon

**River Mile:** 220—right
**Time:** 40 minutes to the Tapeats fall and back
**Difficulty:** Easy to Moderate. Boulder hopping and some 3rd class scrambling.
**Wet or Dry?:** Dry
**Ideal Weather:** Cool
**Potential:** A couple hours of hiking would likely lead to big Redwall amphitheaters at the head of the drainage.
**Camp:** There are three camps at the mouth of 220 Mile.

**Route Description:** A trio of camps at 220 Mile serve as popular last night destinations for trips taking out at Diamond Creek. If you happen to be camped here and can pull yourself away from the party, 220 Mile is a worthwhile hike.

The highlight of lower 220 Mile is a smooth conglomerate bedrock that occasionally surfaces in the creekbed. A wide range of colored cobbles pattern themselves throughout the white mother rock, and the entire matrix has a polished smooth finish. The stuff would make a neat patio floor. Look for this beautiful rock underfoot when it replaces the large gravels that normally fill the creekbed.

As you march upstream, the granite geology gives way to Tapeats Sandstone, which forms a 25-foot fall about 1 mile up from the river. There is a 4th class scramble up the face of this fall, or an easy route around it just downstream on creek left. This fall serves as the standard turnaround spot for the hike. Above the Tapeats fall, the canyon is open, as is typical of drainages in the lower end of the Canyon. The creekbed continues its climb into the Bright Angel Shale before reaching a major fork. This is as far as my explorations have reached. More open hiking above the fork would likely lead to Redwall amphitheaters. According to Harvey Butchart's *Grand Canyon Treks*, there is no route through the Redwall here. He reports: "I entered Two Hundred and Twenty Mile Canyon and concluded that there is no way to get up the Redwall there."

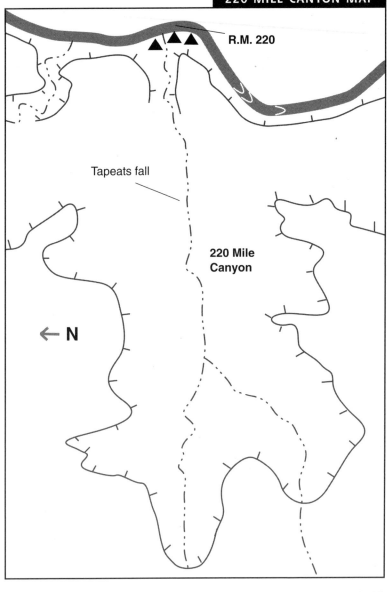

R.M. 220

Tapeats fall

220 Mile
Canyon

← N

1/4 mile

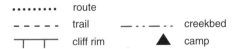

......... route

– – – – trail   –·–·–·– creekbed

┬──┬── cliff rim   ▲ camp

172

Hanging out in 220 Mile Canyon

# Diamond Peak

**River Mile:** 223.5—left
**Time:** 4 to 6 hours to the summit and back
**Difficulty:** Difficult
**Wet or Dry?:** Dry
**Ideal Weather:** Cool
**Potential:** You can make this a one-way hike by walking from Diamond Peak directly to the take out.
**Camp:** There is a medium-sized camp at the mouth of 224 Mile Canyon, which is the start of the hike.

**Route Description:** Normally the routine for take out day is: get to Diamond Creek, load the truck, and get the hell out of there. If you can delay the take out chaos, however, a hike up Diamond Peak is a really cool way to say goodbye to the big ditch. If you are continuing on to Lake Mead, the summit of Diamond Peak offers good views of where you've been and where you're going.

The summit is reached via a 1.5 mile approach hike, followed by 500 feet of scrambling up sharp loose Redwall Limestone. The hike starts at the head of 224 Mile Rapid. From here, you'll walk up the mostly dry creekbed of 224 Mile Canyon for 0.4 miles before veering right (creek left) at a fork. This is the first major drainage entering 224 Mile Canyon on creek left. Follow this gulch about 1,000 vertical feet up to the saddle to the east of Diamond Peak. From the saddle, there is a nice view of the river to the north, and the winding Diamond Creek road to the south.

To the west is the hulk of Diamond Peak. Studying its eastern face, you may not immediately see a route through the steep broken Redwall, but as you climb, you will find that it is not as steep as it looks.

Starting at the saddle, walk up the obvious talus slope to its top. Here, you might see a cairn indicating one of several routes up through the loose gullies and broken boulders above. Continue straight on up, and before long you will be walking the final sharp slope to one of the two summit areas. If the climbing exceeds 4th class, you've picked an unnecessarily difficult route. All the routes are characterized by scrambling over loose sharp rocks.

The summit areas are connected by a narrow ridge with big exposure on its western side. The southern summit is highest at 3,512 feet. The river is over 2,000 feet below, at an elevation of 1,335 feet.

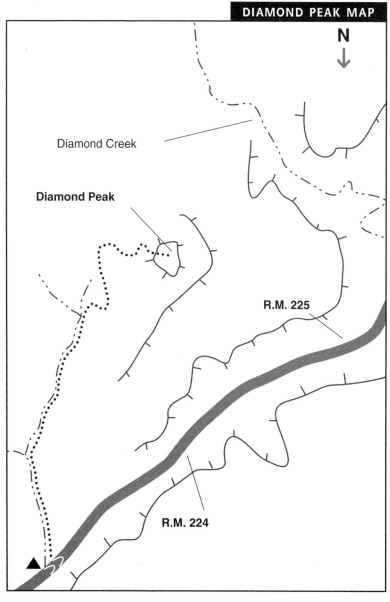

# DIAMOND PEAK MAP

N
↓

Diamond Creek

**Diamond Peak**

**R.M. 225**

**R.M. 224**

1/4 mile

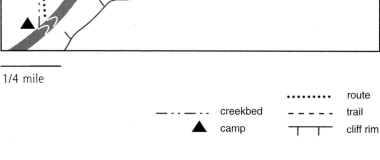

·—··—··— creekbed
▲ camp

•••••••• route
– – – – trail
⊤—⊤—⊤ cliff rim

The summit of Diamond Peak with the Diamond Creek road in the background

# Travertine Canyon

**River Mile:** 229—left
**Time:** 30 minutes to see the waterfall and narrow canyon at the mouth. 2 to 3 hours to go to the springs and back.
**Difficulty:** Moderate
**Wet or Dry?:** Wet
**Ideal Weather:** Any
**Potential:** A hike to the springs leads to the Tonto platform above the inner gorge. There are many hiking options from here.
**Camp:** Several flat sandy areas that could serve as camps are hidden among the boulders near the mouth of Travertine Canyon. However, the flat spots are 20 feet above the river and boat parking here is lousy.

**Route Description:** Travertine Canyon is home to a substantial stream that begins at a large set of springs two miles from the Colorado. Just before the creek empties into the river, it goes over a 35-foot waterfall and through a slot canyon of travertine. A short scramble into the travertine narrows below the waterfall is the standard hike here.

From the river, you'll head upstream along the creek for about 100 yards before being forced to make a scramble over some smooth sloping schist on creek left. If you make it up the sloping schist, you shouldn't have any trouble making the next short climb leading into the narrows. The narrows are short but sweet. A 40-yard-long cave-like travertine slot is backed by a beautiful 35-foot waterfall. In the summer, you won't want to leave this shadowy wet room, but if you are so inclined, there is hiking upstream that is also interesting.

To explore above the travertine box canyon, return to the river and head up the ridge on creek right. There is a cairned route here that leads back into the creek just above the waterfall via a 4th class climb down schist. Once back in the creek, the walking is relatively easy, with the exception of two short waterfall scrambles and a third larger waterfall. At this larger waterfall, you'll have to make it up a 5.3 (15 feet exposure) climb on creek left to continue. The next major obstacle is a thick and unfriendly jungle of riparian vegetation signaling nearness of the springs and a good turnaround spot. You might want to make a short hike to the top of the Tapeats for a slightly better view.

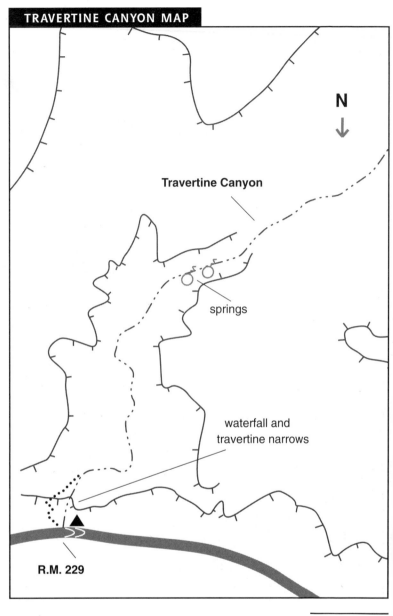

## TRAVERTINE CANYON MAP

N
↓

Travertine Canyon

springs

waterfall and
travertine narrows

R.M. 229

1/4 mile

•••••••• route
– – – – trail          —··—··— creekbed
┬─┬─┬ cliff rim        ▲ camp

Peering out of the Travertine narrows

# Bridge Canyon

**River Mile:** 235.2—left
**Time:** 30 minutes to the bridge and back
**Difficulty:** Easy
**Wet or Dry:?** Wet
**Ideal Weather:** Any
**Potential:** There are numerous routes through the Tapeats in upper Bridge, offering extensive hiking options above the inner gorge.
**Camp:** There is a large camp here and a small one. The small one has the best boat parking. It is above the rapid on the left. The bigger camp is halfway down the rapid on the left.

**Route Description:** There is something here for every Grand Canyon hiker. If you have an itch for exploration, Bridge Canyon leads to open country above the inner gorge perfect for a death march. On the other hand, if you want a simple 30-minute walk to a unique sight, Bridge has that, too.

The most common hike here is upstream to the bridge that gives this canyon its name. There is a trail leading out the back of camp into the heavily vegetated creekbed of Bridge. Hiking here would be reduced to serious bushwhacking were it not for the trail, so it behooves you to stay on it. It leads across the stream a few times before arriving at the natural bridge about 0.4 miles from the river. The small conglomerate bridge spans a side gully on creek right. In Harvey Butchart's words, it is "rather unimpressive." True, it's nothing terribly dramatic, but it's worth the 10 minute walk from camp.

If you want dramatic scenery, continue hacking up Bridge until the vegetation and the water stop in another 0.3 miles, and then find a route up through the Tapeats Sandstone. There are burro trails traversing the desert slopes above the inner gorge that can provide some relatively easy walking, but watch out for the jumping cholla cactus. Ouch!

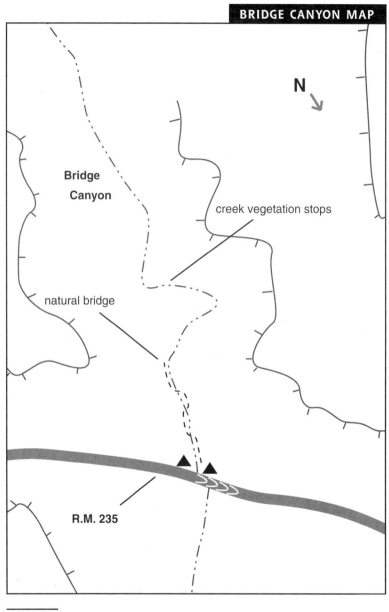

Bridge
Canyon

creek vegetation stops

natural bridge

R.M. 235

N

1/4 mile

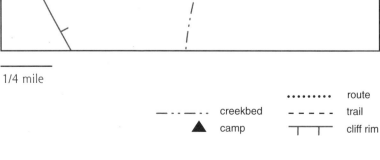

•••••••• route

creekbed          - - - - - trail

▲ camp            cliff rim

Viewing the inner gorge from above Bridge Canyon

# Gneiss Canyon

**River Mile:** 235.8—left
**Time:** 45 minutes round-trip to the first major falls
**Difficulty:** Moderate
**Wet or Dry?:** Wet
**Ideal Weather:** Any
**Potential:** Climbers can make it to upper Gneiss Canyon and on to the Tonto platform.
**Camp:** There is a small to medium camp here, and a larger camp across the river.

**Route Description:** There are a couple of good reasons to stop and hike at Gneiss Canyon. First, there is fantastically-swirled bedrock here displaying some of nature's finest artwork. Second, the river below this point soon becomes the flat monotonous growth of upper Reservoir Mead. Here at Gneiss Canyon it is still a real river—enjoy it while you can.

The best scenery in Gneiss Canyon is near the mouth. Smooth metamorphic rock is spun in creamy patterns. Small pools are linked by trickling waterslides. To get around these pools will require some fancy footwork. Remember the circle-run at Silver Grotto? You'll get to practice it again here. Of course there is also the more conservative wade-through-the-slimy-pool approach.

A good turnaround spot is a 50-foot fall about 0.5 miles up from the river. There is a pretty little pool at the base of the falls that is, well, nice. Sorry I just had to say it.

If you really must see what's up around the bend, a 4th class climb leads up the creek-right side of the falls. At the top you'll be greeted with an even higher waterfall. To get around these falls, look for a climbing route on creek left. It is a 5.4 climb on slightly rotten rock with enough exposure to kill you. Needless to say, it's scary.

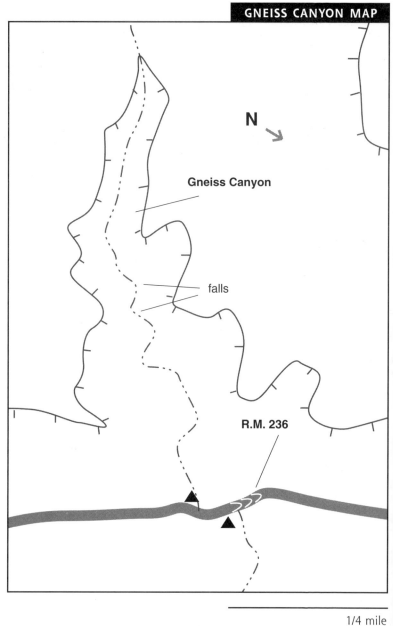

Gneiss Canyon

falls

N

R.M. 236

1/4 mile

......... route

- - - - - trail          —··—··— creekbed

┬──┬──┬ cliff rim        ▲ camp

This is not sandal country

# Separation Canyon

**River Mile:** 239.5—right
**Time:** 1 to 2 hours for a 2-mile round-trip up the canyon
**Difficulty:** Easy
**Wet or Dry?:** Wet. The easiest walking is in the creek.
**Ideal Weather:** Cool or Moderate
**Potential:** Lots. Ask the Howland brothers.
**Camp:** There is a medium-sized camp at Separation.

**Route Description:** This is the place where Oramel Howland, Seneca Howland, and William Dunn made their fatal decision to hike out of the Canyon in 1869. The fearsome rapid that helped their decision is gone now, but the canyon country they walked into is still much the same. For history buffs, this is a good place to walk in the footsteps of our predecessors and try to imagine what it was like a century and a half ago.

From the sandy beach at the mouth of Separation, there is a trail that skirts the mud of the creek bottom by crossing the desert slope on creek right. Within 100 yards, you'll be weaving through the riparian vegetation of the creekbed on your way upstream. About a quarter-mile from the river, water springs up, providing a natural walkway clear of vegetation. A little over a mile from the river, the creek hides under the gravels once again, leaving a more open desert wash. This canyon is big, wide, and straight, lending quick access to the backcountry of the Sanup Plateau region.

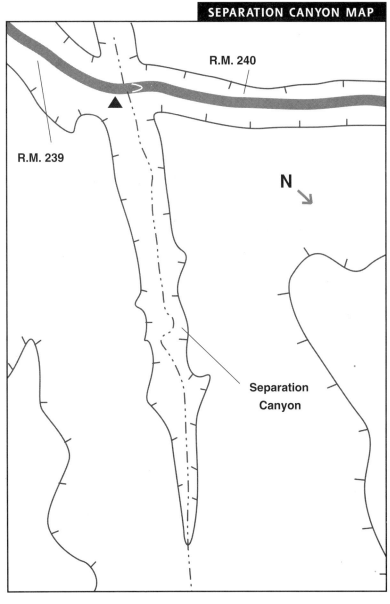

## SEPARATION CANYON MAP

R.M. 240

R.M. 239

N

Separation
Canyon

1/4 mile

route

creekbed          trail

camp              cliff rim

Separation Canyon is still much like it was in 1869.

# Spencer Canyon

**River Mile:** 246—left
**Time:** 5 to 8 hours to go to the Meriwhitica junction and back
**Difficulty:** Moderate
**Wet or Dry?:** Wet
**Ideal Weather:** Moderate
**Potential:** Spencer Canyon continues for great distances with nothing to stop you but your energy level.
**Camp:** There is a big beach camp at Spencer when the water is low; otherwise, it's sparse accommodations. Separation has a decent camp 6 miles upstream.

**Route Description:** Spencer Canyon is a huge drainage in empty country. You might forget that you are in Grand Canyon with Spencer's clear stream and polished granite boulders, but when you glance up to see Redwall cliffs three thousand feet above, you'll remember.

The mouth of Spencer Canyon is a jungle of willow, cottonwood, cattail, and tamarisk. Walking through this morass can be hard work. You may even find yourself asking: What the hell am I doing here? I did. However, a little perseverance will soon have you a quarter mile from the river and out of the jungle. Generally the best way to get through this first part is straight up the creek, although you might have to skirt a couple of deep pools.

The broad canyon meanders upstream for a little over three miles before a fork in the streambed indicates Meriwhitica Canyon entering on creek left. The water and Spencer Canyon continue straight ahead to Spencer Springs in another mile—a good turnaround point.

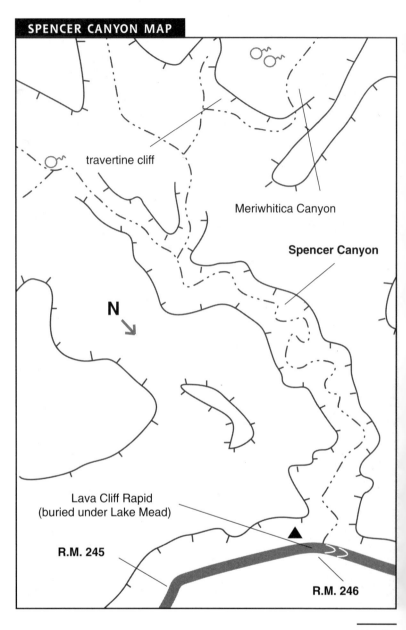

## SPENCER CANYON MAP

travertine cliff

Meriwhitica Canyon

**Spencer Canyon**

N

Lava Cliff Rapid
(buried under Lake Mead)

**R.M. 245**

**R.M. 246**

1/4 mile

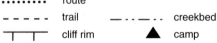

......... route
- - - - - trail ─ ·· ─ ·· ─ creekbed
┬┬┬┬ cliff rim ▲ camp

Dense vegetation often covers the mouth of Spencer Canyon.

# Columbine Falls (Cave Canyon)

**River Mile:** 274.2—left
**Time:** 1.5 hours to the head of the narrows and back
**Difficulty:** Moderate to Difficult. Getting into the canyon is a heinous task.
**Wet or Dry?:** Wet
**Ideal Weather:** Any
**Potential:** Cave Canyon looks quite intriguing from the map, with possible routes to the top of the Grand Wash Cliffs.
**Camp:** There are two camps just downstream from here, at the back of small bays.

**Route Description:** Just before rounding the corner of the Grand Wash Cliffs into the empty and warm waters of Reservoir Mead, there is one last Grand Canyon hike that is definitely worth a visit. Cave Canyon dumps into Lake Mead over a beautiful streaking waterfall called Columbine (some call it Emery) Falls. Above this waterfall, Cave Canyon is a boulder-studded Eden with a clear trickling stream, maidenhair ferns, and copious green and red monkey flowers. It is reminiscent of another place in Grand Canyon known as Elves Chasm.

To get into the canyon, you must ascend the slope a couple hundred yards out from the falls, and then traverse toward the top of the falls, approaching from creek left. There is a crude trail making this traverse through muddy sawgrass and across sharp travertine boulders. The trail improves the hiking from totally heinous to rough. Once you find yourself on the travertine bluff above the waterfall, look for a route into the creekbed. There is no easy or good way. I finally settled on a steep, loose gully that terminates directly at the top of the waterfall and uncomfortably close to the edge.

Once you've made the rugged scramble into the creekbed, things improve dramatically. Fun boulder scrambles link lovely clear pools trimmed by maidenhair ferns for the first 200 yards upstream. Then, just when you've seen all the monkey flowers you can stand, smooth walls of limestone close in, replacing the Elves Chasm scenery with something more similar to Matkatamiba. The narrows continue for about a quarter-mile, then the water disappears, and the canyon opens up.

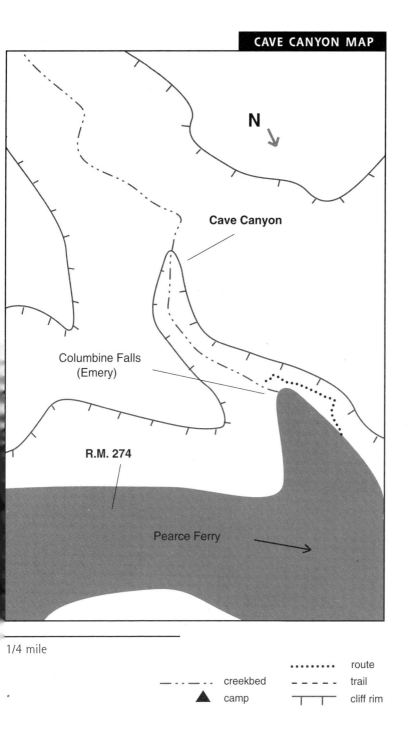

N

**Cave Canyon**

Columbine Falls
(Emery)

**R.M. 274**

Pearce Ferry

1/4 mile

| | | |
|---|---|---|
| — · · — · · — | creekbed | · · · · · · · · route |
| ▲ camp | | – – – – trail |
| | | ⊤—⊤—⊤ cliff rim |

Cave Canyon

# Shops, Products, and Services

196